Donna Sue's Down Home Trailer Park Bartending Guide

Donna Sue Boxcar

Foreword by Ruby Ann Boxcar

CITADEL PRESS
Kensington Publishing Corp.
www.kensingtonbooks.com

For Ruby, I ate your dust, and followed it with a double vodka stinger.
Thanks for revealin' all my personal secrets in your books.
Now, go choke on a beer nut.

CITADEL PRESS books are published by

Kensington Publishing Corp.
850 Third Avenue
New York, NY 10022

All Kensington titles, imprints, and distributed lines are available at special quantity discounts for bulk purchases for sales promotions, premiums, fund-raising, educational, or institutional use. Special book excerpts or customized printings can also be created to fit specific needs. For details, write or phone the office of the Kensington special sales manager: Kensington Publishing Corp., 850 Third Avenue, New York, NY 10022, attn: Special Sales Department, phone 1-800-221-2647.

Citadel Press logo Reg. U.S. Patent and Trademark Office
Citadel Press is a trademark of Kensington Publishing Corp.

The following are trademarks of their respective owners, who do not endorse this book: Dr Pepper, Everclear, Jell-O, Mad Dog 20/20, 7UP, Hot Damn, Oreo, RC Cola, Red Hots, and Lipton

First printing: September 2003

10 9 8 7 6 5 4 3 2 1

Printed in the United States of America

Library of Congress Control Number: 2003103628

ISBN: 0-8065-2565-7

This book is intended for entertainment purposes only. Neither the author nor the publisher will assume responsibility for the use or misuse of any information contained within this book.

Contents

Acknowledgments

I'd like to thank momma and daddy for believin' in me and lovin' me no matter what.

I love you dearly—and by the way, I've already picked out your room at the Last Stop Nursing Home, where you'll be spendin' your final days. As for the rest of my family, I love ya'll too, but the rules still stand: "Don't wake me before noon, stay out of my liquor cabinet, I won't loan you any money, and no, you can't borrow the Bonneville."

Thanks to my sister, Ruby Ann, for encouragin' me to write about things I know. I wouldn't have this opportunity if you hadn't said, "Donna, get your drunk butt up, send that man home, and write down them drinks." I've always been jealous of your abilities. But on behalf of a grateful nation, thanks for not goin' into strippin'. Lord, I need a drink just to get that picture out of my mind.

I'm grateful to my sister Ruby's musical director, Robert Brown, who also happens to be my good friend and business consultant for twenty years. (And thanks for turning me on to Gold Bond Medicated Powder.)

I owe a great deal of thanks to thank Mr. Curtis Moore for being my exotic dance choreographer, without whom I might still be workin' that dive in Chicago, Oklahoma, and gettin' paid with free beer.

My thanks to Kevin Wiley for keepin' my hair and makeup lookin' good on all my personal appearances and such—I'm still tryin to get you hired on at the Beauty Barge. I also want to thank Wiley Designs for all the great clothes and purses that depict the core of my style and sensuousness.

My thanks to Margaret, Joan, Mary, Laurie, Kris, and Tareth for all your help and for stayin' away from my men.

I'd like to give a special thanks to Walter, Steven, Bruce, and Doug for all your support, and for undressin' me with your eyes every time we were in a room together. (It's too bad I don't mix business with pleasure.)

My thanks to all the rest of the gang at Citadel/Kensington. I'd come see you more often, but ever since that elevator incident for some reason I can't get by security.

Thanks to George for catching the essence of pure loveliness and beauty that is me, in the photo on the cover of my book.

Thanks to my good friend and co-worker, Little Linda, for headlinin' at the club while I'm away.

And finally, I'd like to give a special thanks to the girls, staff, and customers at the Blue Whale. Contrary to the rumors, I'll be back soon, and I ain't got too good to make change for a dollar on stage.

Foreword

Seein' how I was the baby of the family, I was always bein' compared to my older brother or sister. I can't tell you how many times people would hold me up to the light that Jack Daniels or Donna Sue had put off as they grew up ahead of me. My teachers would always point out to the class how better my brother was at spellin', how quicker my sister had learned to write, how higher Donna Sue could jump, or how fast Jack Daniels could swim. What they neglected to add was that my brother couldn't pronounce his own name till he was seven years old, my sister couldn't tell the difference between an adverb and a noun till ninth grade, jumpin' Donna Sue wasn't wearin' a DD bra by the time she was eleven, and Jack Daniel's quick aquatic abilities were on account of the fact that he'd been born with freakish ducklike webbed feet and hands. Oh no, those facts weren't important enough to be brought up durin' my public admonishment. But don't get me wrong, I'm not bitter. As a matter of fact, I always enjoyed bein' compared to my older sister. Not only was she smart and gifted, but she also had a dream.

Donna Sue had always wanted to be a nurse. She had this longin' deep down inside her to help and to comfort others. When any of us in the family would get ill or sick, she'd be right there by our sides doin' what she could to heal us back to health. Yes, dear readers, even when we would treat her rudely on account of our illness, my lovin' sister would set right there by our sick bed and take it. Truly she was the Florence Nightingale of The High Chaparral Trailer Park in Pangburn, Arkansas.

When it came to school, she was a straight A student who never missed a day of class. She was always there and ready to learn. And the scholastic awards that she'd achieved took up two full walls in the livin' room of

Momma and Daddy's trailer. With her brains and her dreams there was nothin' that could hold Donna Sue back from bein' a nurse. Or so we thought.

Donna Sue's graduation from high school was truly a day of celebration in the Boxcar family. On account of my brother's droppin' out to follow his dream of bein' a finger puppeteer (that dream was quickly squashed on account of his weak knuckle joints), my sister was the first one of us kids to receive a high school diploma. She was also the first Boxcar ever to head off to college. Yes, in less than a week my sister would be attendin' the WestArk School of Nursin' in Fort Smith. At least that was the plan before the surprise graduation party that my folks had put together for Donna Sue down at Pangburn's Dream Cream. But that path and my sister's life would all be altered on that night by a simple gesture of love from my Pa-Pa. As you might have guessed, my sister had been a clean-cut kid with no drinkin', smokin', or even occasional boyfriend to get in her way to success. So when Pa-Pa toasted her for bringin' pride to our clan's name, the beer he gave her was in all actuality her very first drop of liquor. Long story short, she loved it. After just one bottle of brew this sister that I'd grown up with changed right before my eyes. Her staunch conservatism and want to be a nurse slid by the roadside with each sip of the devil's drink. That day would be the last time I ever saw her sober. By mornin' Donna Sue had chosen a new road to travel, a new tree to climb, a new bull to ride. From that day on my sister would be a professional drunk.

Almost forty years have passed since that night, and my sister is still two sheets to the wind. Don't get me wrong, she's not always fall-down drunk. Typically she is simply tipsy, but still able to function. She continues to drive, but only when she is under the legal intoxication limit—or so she says. Daddy installed a device in her Bonneville that won't allow her to start the car if it detects more than the allowed amount of alcohol on her breath, but she's found ways to get around that by usin' other parts of her body to blow into the tube. (She gets great gas mileage when she does it that way, but the car exhaust will kill you.) I also want you to understand that Donna Sue isn't an alcoholic either. She drinks because she likes the way it makes her feel.

As far as her career goes, my sister has found a line of work that still allows her to give comfort to others and drink all at the same time. She's an exotic dancer. Yes, now in her late fifties, Donna Sue still packs 'em in at The Blue Whale Strip Club in Searcy, Arkansas. She also sits by her customer's beds from time to time like she use to sit by ours. And yes, she still takes it. Her life has allowed her to help those who need it. She's also able to touch people like she never would've been able to as a nurse. And thanks to her many years of drinkin' she can honestly make some of the best drinks you've ever had.

It was because of this later fact that I encouraged my slightly inebriated sister to write down some of her stories and share her vast library of adult beverages with you, the payin' public. With that in mind, ladies and gentlemen, boys and girls of all ages, I now proudly give you my dear sister, Donna Sue Boxcar, and her collection of concoctions.

RUBY ANN BOXCAR

Who'd have thought that one day this young petite thing would turn into the sexy beast of love and drink mixologist that I've become today?

Preface

Well, here I am, Donna Sue Boxcar with my very own bartendin' guide. Now maybe you're wonderin', who is this gal? Well, you may know me on account of my sister, Ruby Ann Boxcar, being a famous author of *Ruby Ann's Down Home Trailer Park Cookbook, Ruby Ann's Down Home Trailer Park Holiday Guide,* and *Ruby Ann's Down Home Trailer Park BBQin' Cookbook*—and also an entertainer and temptress of song—mentionin' about me and my dancin' in her books.

As my sister told you in the foreword of this book, I'd wanted to be a nurse. But instead, I chose a different path. I was meant to ease the pain and sufferin' of this world, and I found that I could still comfort people and make them feel better by bein' an exotic dancer.

Once I tasted liquor at my graduation party, I knew then that unless nursin' involved drinkin' (which I think they frown on), it was not for me. No, nursin' was out, and I had to figure out how to party and make a livin' at it. While I was partyin' and drinkin' at a friend's trailer with some newly released prisoners we had just picked up hitchhikin', it came to me. I had a big-gal body, natural rhythm, and I was born to boogie. I was up on the coffee table dancin' and carryin' on like usual, when the boys started givin' me drinks, tippin' me cigarettes, and askin' me to take my clothes off. They were really feelin' good watchin' me dance and strip and I knew I'd found my callin'. Free drinks for takin' off my clothes? And they all enjoyed it so much, how could I disappoint 'em? Now all I had to do was find a place that would pay me for it. Which brought me to the idea of becomin' an exotic dancer and stripper.

I joined the stripper circuit and have been bumpin' and grindin' for nearly four decades. I've taken my clothes off more times than Anna

Nicole Smith at an AARP convention. I have worked the stripper circuit all over the country and had drinks in every bar. When it comes to drinks, I've tried 'em all, and bartenders ask *me* for recipes.

I love the taste of a delicious cocktail. Now, don't get me wrong there are other things I enjoy in life, like bingo, travel, food, bowlin', and cookin', and I really love men, but most of all I love drinkin'. And when it comes to experience with liquor, I've got more than Foster Brooks, W. C. Fields, Ted Kennedy, or even the Bush girls put together.

Unlike many who have written bartendin' guides in the past, I have spent most of my wakin' hours over the last thirty-nine years or so conductin' unbiased tests and thorough research in the field of drinkin'. I have sampled practically every adult beverage known to man or woman. Not only that, but I love olives and other drink garnishes, and before my trailer burnt, I had the largest known collection of drink umbrellas and swizzle sticks in Arkansas.

Now you may ask what sets my book apart from all those other cocktail guides on the market? Well, do those other guides tell you how to make a good Dr Pepper Martini or a Skid Mark? I doubt it. You won't find drinks like Arkansas Antifreeze or Stripper's Zipper in them big-city bartendin' books. You just ask them Yankee bartenders if they know how to make an Oklahoma Tornado or a Backseat Boogie, and they'll look at you like you gave 'em a pop quiz in shop class.

Sure, we southerners drink exotic cocktails, like a Mountain Sunset, a Funky Monkey, or the infamous Viagra Please!, but I've got the real recipes for the down-home drinks we have all come to know and love. I'm sure you'll find somethin' you like. You may want to try the Arkansas Roadkill, Gutter Trash, Sewer Water, Deferred Sentence, Lucifer's Lap Dance, or Thunder Thong, which we named in my fellow dancer, Edna Rotoweeder's honor on account of how long she was off with that bad thong burn.

I hope you'll enjoy the stories I have collected about all the wonderful people I consider to be my family at The Blue Whale Strip Club. And I'm gonna give you some of my personal tips about drinkin' and makin' drinks, as well as tips from the girls.

Now, as an added bonus I have shared with you my favorite shots and shooters, frozen concoctions, punches and party potions, and even homemade liquor. And I've thrown in some of our favorite food recipes from the menu of the Blue Whale to help with your entertainin' at parties.

I've tried to make my bartendin' guidebook an easy-to-read-and-use road map to creatin' delicious libations that even the novice party-giver can follow. I'll tell you what you need to set up your bar, and how to mix it the easy way. You don't even have to have any fancy liqueurs or mixes. You can use plain old Dr Pepper, Mountain Dew, and Kool-Aid to make some great drinks. For example, for a Dover Clover you only need vodka, lemon-lime Kool-Aid, and 7UP. I also use my own Homemade Sweet 'n' Sour Mix instead of store-bought, but your choice can be your call.

You don't have to be so doggone exact about your measurin' either—a mouthful or three fingers ought to get it about right—but for some of you nervous Nellys out there I did put in measurements. You don't even have to have all them fancy liquors, 'cause I have recipes to make quite a few at home. And keep in mind that each recipe in the book makes one drink unless another yield is given.

Somethin' else you won't find in them highfalutin' books are my personal memories and thoughts that head up each of the chapters, includin' wine and beers. Plus I give y'all a brief history on how each liquor is made, which gives you somethin' to share with your fellow patrons at the bar. I follow this up with one of my personal quotes on the subject and then we dive right into the drinks and/or food recipes, whichever the case might be.

But before we get started, I want to talk to y'all about a serious subject: drinkin' is fun, but please, whatever you do, **DON'T DRINK AND DRIVE**. I've got lots more books I want to share with y'all and I'd like to have you around to enjoy them. If you're gonna drink, make sure you give your keys to a friend, call a taxi, or just spend the night at a motel or with a friend, or at a motel with a "friend."

So have a good time, and, as I always say, *"MAY YOUR GLASS ALWAYS BE FULL AND YOUR BOTTOM UP."*

Introduction

If these walls could talk, well, I'd be in a lot of trouble.

The Blue Whale Strip Club
"Who's Who" and What They Do

THE BLUE WHALE GIRLS

Our exotic dancers

Ms. Donna Sue

Y'all already know about me, and that I'm the headliner. Of course I'm also the emcee or hostess, I work behind the bar from time to time, and when Mildred's arthritis or gout flares up, I also play the music so me and my fellow entertainers can do our exotic dancin'. Oh yes, and if you buy a bowl of your favorite shelled nuts, I come by and break the shells off for you. As a matter of fact, you can order online a souvenir T-shirt on the Blue Whale Strip Club page that says "Donna Sue Cracked My Nuts." Ain't that nice? (The Web address is near the end of this section, just keep readin'.)

Somethin' you may not know about me is that I am also a business-woman. If you check out my sister's book on BBQin', you can read all about my pawnshop, and I have recently started a new business: Wienies on Wheels, a travelin' hot dog stand that you can hook up with a bumper hitch to your vehicle. I got the idea while eatin' a wienie and watchin' an ice cream truck go by. Mind you, I love ice cream, but I would chase a truck down for a big hot wienie any day. Now my business covers certain parts of Arkansas, and franchises are available in west Tennessee and other parts of the south if you're interested.

I rent franchises to the girls at the Blue Whale, but I divide out the territories so none of the girls are workin' each other's corners. Now, I have some rules for my girls.

1. I get a percentage of everything they take in.
2. I have some of my boyfriends watch the carts so the girls aren't skimmin' off the top. (The skin on the top of the wienie water is what gives them cheap wienies their fine flavor.)
3. I look out for my girls, and I keep an attorney on call in case the girls are ever arrested for solicitin' wienies without a license.
4. I also tell them to never touch them wienies without puttin' on their rubber gloves first.

I also rent out wienie wagons for school and church fund-raisers, so if you wanna make some extra cash, you need to call me and I'll set you up with all the wienies you can handle.

You know when there is somethin' special goin' on in town 'cause you'll see me drivin' down the street with several wienie wagons behind my Bonneville. I can tow up to five at a time before the police get onto me. Most times they let me go if I give 'em a coupon for a freebie and a bag of Lay's.

Every once in a while you will know when I've had a little bit too much to drink. I have been told that one time I was standin' on a corner at four A.M. hollerin', "Get your wienies hot here!" The problem was I didn't have a cart with me.

And one time after work, I didn't even know it but I had one of the wagons behind my old car and was in a hurry to get home and clean up my trailer before my gentlemen friend came over. I was turnin' corners practically on two wheels. When I got home I realized I was draggin' one of them carts behind me, and it was upside down shootin' sparks all the way down the street. There were loose wienies all over town.

Recently after a trip to New York I was inspired to add roasted nuts machines to all my wienie wagons to serve on cold fall and winter evenings. I don't know about you, but there's nothin' will arouse your appetite more than the smell of a hot wienie, unless it's the aroma of some warm nuts.

Also, don't forget to come and visit me on my Web page. Just go to my sister's site at www.donnasueboxcar.com. Make sure you drop me an e-mail or at least take the time to sign my guest book, 'cause you know I love each and every one of you. And if you send me a picture of yourself, I'll send you a picture of me if I can get that dang camera to focus. Anyhow, let's meet the rest of the Blue Whales.

Ms. Edna Rotoweeder

We are proud to have Ms. Edna back with our cast. As many of you regulars know, Edna left our lineup last year after a terrible bout of heat rash and an unusual case of thong burn. Well, the good news is that she beat the rash and is back better then ever. Edna had hoped her new set of dentures would be here for our December shows, but they've got lost in the mail. God bless her, she certainly has had problems tryin' to get those mail-order teeth. Why, just this past November when a package did arrive at the club for her, we were sure her luck had changed. She opened that package like it was Christmas and sure enough there were her choppers. Immediately she took those things and shoved 'em in her mouth, and then gave us this great big smile. I couldn't believe how beautiful she was. It was purely amazin'. But that beauty didn't stay very long, for just seconds later she spit those teeth onto the table and began rubbin' her tongue and scrunchin' up her face as if she'd eaten a stick of deodorant. When she could finally speak, she said somethin' nasty tastin' was on those teeth, and that her tongue and gums were numb. Well when we looked inside the packet, sure enough there was a white powdery substance, which of course set off warnin' signs inside our heads. Immediately we called Sheriff Gentry, who in turn called out one of them teams of fellas who dress up in them big spaceman-lookin' outfits. They came and treated Edna, took her teeth and the package, and quarantined everyone in The Blue Whale Strip Club. Well, thank goodness our luck had held out and the angels were with us that day. You see, just moments before that stupid package had arrived, the liquor man had dropped off his delivery of booze, so we was trapped in the club with a fully stocked bar. I tell you, sometimes you just feel blessed, don't you? Anyhow, gettin' back to the story, it turned out that the powder was nothin' more than industrial-strength rat poison, thank the Lord, and that all of us girls were just fine. Of course Edna had to spend a few days in intensive care down at the hospital, and her teeth and that package were handed over to the district attorney as evidence. He's pressin' charges against the company in Taiwan who makes and distributes the dentures with incompetence, neglect, and attempted manslaughter. But he assures Edna that she'll get her teeth back just as soon as the case is over, which with all the red tape they have to go through on account of it's bein' a company in another country and all, she'll see those teeth of hers sometime in 2005. Welcome back, Edna, we love you.

Ms. Ila LaFleur

Just 'cause Ms. Ila "Flossy" LaFleur now calls Happy Dreams Retirement Center her new home doesn't mean she is ready to pack up her feather boa and pasties. As a matter of fact, she says now that she's got that new hip and knee, she feels better than ever. For those new to the world of exotic dancin', Flossy (as we Blue Whale girls call her) has been a star in this business for years. She's gotten to the ripe old age of eighty-four, and she started strippin' back in 1932 at the tender age of thirteen. Her first strip-tease was purely by accident. You see, while she was attendin' a political rally for a man who was runnin' for office, a bee flew right under her dress. Well, as this politician was right in the middle of his speech on why voters should vote for him, Flossy let out this blood-curdlin' scream and started jumpin' all around tryin' to get that dang bee out of her clothes before it stung her. Filled with utter terror and panic, Flossy started takin' her clothes off until she was standin' there in nothin' but her panties, socks, and shoes. It wasn't until the loud roar of laughter hit her like the 3:15 train to Cincinnati that she realized she was standin' almost naked in a crowd of over three hundred folks. Utterly embarrassed, Flossy grabbed her clothes and began to cry. As she quickly got dressed, her tears turned into an all-out bawlin'. It was then that this fella, whose speech had been interrupted, called her up to the stage. Flossy was so humiliated that she simply turned around and tried to run away, but the people in attendance wouldn't let her go. Instead they passed little thirteen-year-old Ila LaFleur all the way up to the stage, where this politician took her in his warm arms and told her that she shouldn't be upset. As he held her tightly he went on to tell her and the crowd in attendance that this little girl was just like our country as it fought to survive from the economic depression. He said that good folks had been forced to strip away their pride until they too were like this dear one, frightened and embarrassed. Anyhow, the fella went on to turn it into a "vote for me speech," and after it was all over, he gave Flossy a ride to her house, and a whole quarter so she could buy candy. That was Flossy's first tip, and that man was Franklin D. Roosevelt, who did win his election that year. Flossy didn't actually get into dancin' until she was seventeen, but she did get to see President Roosevelt again in 1942 when, after she wrote a letter to him recallin' the incident, he invited her to join him at the White House for a little visit. He was wonderful to her, but when she tried to dance for the president, his Scottie dog, Fala, kept barkin' at her and even tried to nip her once or twice as she unbuttoned her top.

Of course, nothin's changed when it comes to our dear Flossy. Men are still givin' her quarters and dogs still bark at her, and the old girl still takes it off six nights a week. She tells anyone who will listen that as long as she can "squat down on a table and manage to get back up" or "not trip over my own breast," you'll be able to find her up on a stage. Not bad for a gal who leaves every night with her twenty-two-year-old boyfriend named Digger. So come on in and see Flossy. And don't be surprised if she sort of quotes her favorite president just before she starts to take her clothes off, by sayin', "The only thing you have to fear is fear itself! So grab that bag of quarters and come on down!"

Little Linda

Thanks to your cards and letters to the Arkansas State Parole Board, Little Linda is back with our cast of girls! It goes to show that not even the accidental shootin' of a security guard durin' a botched bank robbery can keep a talented gal down . . . at least not for long.

As many of y'all who attend The Blue Whale Strip Club on a regular basis already know, everybody's favorite big girl has seen her troubles with the law. For some reason Little Linda, who, other than me, happens to get the most repeat customers for our shows, just can't seem to live the straight and narrow. It seems like every week she's in handcuffs and five or six times a year those handcuffs belong to the police. I don't know if she does some of the crazy lawless things that she does on account of her weight (362 pounds) or if it's just 'cause she's a spur-of-the-moment kind of gal, but she just can't seem to go a year without endin' up in jail for somethin' stupid. And I ought to know, I've bailed her out more times than George W. has mispronounced words. Little Linda, who is a barrel of fun to hang out with, has seen the inside of a jail cell for everything from shopliftin' to car theft (she tried to steal a Mazda Miata, and would've gotten away with it too, if only she'd been able to get out of the car without us havin' to call in the fire department). And now she can add bank robbery and attempted murder to her 360-mile-long record. Actually they dropped both charges this time around, thanks to your cards, letters, e-mails, and faxes as well as those from many state politicians who happen to enjoy seein' Little Linda strip. By the way, the security guard's family says he is doin' much better, and thanks everyone for their kind well wishes and flowers. His family also says that just as soon as he is able to eat on his own again, he will be joinin' us at The Blue Whale Strip Club to use that coupon we sent him for a free Fish Basket (drinks not included).

After sayin' all that, I do have to tell y'all that Little Linda has taken a step in the right direction, and *is* tryin' to walk the straight and narrow; well, actually she's more along the lines of stumblin' across the straight and narrow: She bought an old houseboat over on the lake just as soon as she was out of jail, and she's converted it into a floatin' hair salon. She's rentin' out stylin' stations to a staff that consists of three beauticians, one makeup gal, and a masseuse. Business was so good in just the first few weeks that she was forced to buy a junket boat, attach it to the houseboat, and put in a couple of girls that do nails. Actually they're Siamese twins, Kim and Sue Lee, but let me tell you, these gals can make your nails look like they was born good, if you know what I mean. And with both of 'em workin' on you, you can get your nails done in half the time it normally takes you at any other shop. Of course the only bad thing is you got to double tip 'em, but it's well worth it. So if you're in these parts and need your hair, makeup, or nails done, or even if you'd just like a good rubdown, give 'em a holler over at Little Linda's Beauty Barge and tell 'em Donna Sue sent you. Oh, and don't forget Little Linda will happily validate small boat rentals for one hour with each appointment. And if you're smart, pay with cash only. The last thing you need is for Little Linda to have your checkin' account or credit card number.

In honor of Little Linda's return, we'll be takin' a dime off the price of Jell-O shots and your second body shot from Little Linda is half price. So close your eyes, boys, and bottoms up!

Ms. Amy and Slimy

Ms. Amy has to have one of the most unique acts to ever hit the stage of The Blue Whale Strip Club (we do mean *hit* 'cause sometimes she tends to have a little pick-me-up before she goes on). Personally, I think she has a drinkin' problem, but for some odd reason she won't listen to me when I try to help. She just laughs in my face and tells me that instead of watchin' what she drinks, I should keep an eye on all the booze I pour down *my* throat! But that's the first sign of a drunk, isn't it? Denial. She just don't get it that she's just an exotic dancer who can't control the amount of liquor she drinks, whereas I'm an exotic dancer who also happens to be a professional drinker. Of course it's not just me that's tried to help her, but the rest of the girls as well. And if she wasn't such a good dancer with such a good act, I know Melba would let her go. But what do you expect when a girl like Ms. Amy shares the stage with her pet slug Slimy (sittin' on her right arm). If you're one of those folks who never considered a slug to be erotic, then you ain't seen Ms. Amy and Slimy's act! When asked where she got the idea to use a slug in her show, she recalls the day after a wild night's drunk when she woke up in a strange yard with Slimy crawlin' across her face. She knew then that slug was heaven sent!

So come on down to The Blue Whale Strip Club, and see Ms. Amy and Slimy. But please, just remember that if she asks you to buy her a few drinks, make sure you get her somethin' like three or four glasses of brandy or wine or even beer, but *not* the hard stuff.

Ms. Flora Delight

Our newest cast member, Ms. Flora Delight comes to us all the way from Birmingham, Alabama, where she entertained for the past twenty years at the Strip Emporium and TV Repair Palace. Even though she's an ample age fifty-two, she can still make a man scream with her sensuous dance moves, *and* she can also replace your IC101 microprocessor while solderin' the joint on your CRT socket and changin' out your leaky QX3208, givin' you one of the best pictures that old TV set of yours has ever displayed. Why, while I was doin' an out-of-town guest spot a few years back at the Emporium, I actually watched Flora entice an entire group of French businessmen by dancin' to the Garth Brooks and George Jones song "Beer Run" while she ran a diagnostic test on a forty-two-inch rear projection picture-in-picture Toshiba big screen. It was somethin' to behold. But after me buggin' the heck out of her, Flora decided to take me up on my offer and come on up to Searcy, Arkansas, to join our little group of girls. And, men, to answer the question that I know y'all have been wonderin', yes, she is single (thanks to a recent hit and run) and is lookin' for Mr. Right, Mr. Wrong, or, for that matter, just plain old Mr. Anybody as long as he enjoys laughin', is fun to be with, and don't work at a tollbooth. She can't bear to lose another one on account of bad drivin'.

So make our newest Blue Whale girl feel welcomed, and leave those TVs at home, 'cause she's retired from that line of work. However, busted small appliances are welcome by appointment.

Melba Toast

Even though this RED HOT MOMMA is almost sixty, she is not only one of the highest tipped girls at The Blue Whale Strip Club, ($23 just in loose change alone one Saturday night), but Melba also happens to be the owner along with her old man, chef Bernie D. Toast (see "In the Kitchen"). Melba enjoys gettin' up onstage and dancin' for her man, who watches from the kitchen window over the hot food that he slings out every night, but she'll tell you that bein' a stripper wasn't the life she'd dreamed of as a child. No, this little girl from Mississippi had always wanted to be gospel singer, just like her grandma and aunt. As a matter of fact, when she was just a teenager she was asked to take her ailin' granny's place in the singin' group, which her aunt had founded. And even though it was only for one night, little Melba Crackerbox (her maiden name) lived out her dream and took the stage as one of the Danglin' Berries. Both her Granny Berry and old maid Aunt Eunice Berry agreed that she had talent, but the beautiful voice that came out of her mouth was always distracted by her nervous habit of constantly unbuttonin' and then rebuttonin' the top few buttons on her blouse when she performed in front of people. Yes, even as a teenager, her natural instincts were comin' out.

After graduatin' from high school with honors, Melba shortened her last name to just plain Cracker and moved to Jackson, Mississippi, where she worked a few odd jobs while tryin' to break into modelin'. It wouldn't take long until the big break would come, and by the time she was a mere thirty-two years of age, Melba had appeared in both *Jet* and *Ebony* magazines as a foot model in a series of corn and bunion pad ads. She was on her way to stardom and would soon find her dry rough feet in a large half page ad in *Life* magazine. Melba Cracker, the highest paid foot disorder model in the market, was on top of the world, but before she could say "Epsom salts," her career came crashin' down. It all started with an ingrown toenail and a treatment for a hammertoe. Before Melba knew what had happened, her feet had somehow turned on her. The old dry skin was gone, the fungus had disappeared, and the cracks were miraculously healed. It was as if the good Lord above had given her a sign that it was time to move on. And so she did.

After another concert fillin' in for her granny, thirty-three-year-old Melba would hear somethin' that'd finally get her on the right track. One of the ladies at the concert came up to her and noted how nice it was to finally hear her sing without havin' to watch her play with her buttons. This of course was due to the fact that the Danglin' Berries now wore beautiful purple robes with pink trim, so there were no buttons for Melba to unbutton. "But," the elderly white-haired woman added, "why, with the way you kept liftin' up your robe, you'd have thought you was a stripper, child." It was then that the lightbulb went off in Melba's head. That was what her true callin' was, to be a stripper. And so she went on to spend the next fifteen years travelin' the country usin' the talents that God gave her. And before long every low-life dancer, high-class bumper, and good-time grinder from Little Rock to Boise would be compared to the Red Hot Momma, Ms. Melba Cracker.

And now after years of dancin' and a new husband, Melba Toast is proud to welcome you to her own club, The Blue Whale Strip Club, which she and her husband opened together around twenty years ago. I was honored to have Melba personally select me as her club's headliner, and I got to tell you that there ain't none better than the Toasts when it comes to this business. So please make sure that when you're in the area to stop by for some good food and top-notch exotic dancin', and tell 'em Melba and me sent you.

IN THE KITCHEN

Our cookin' staff

Chef Bernie D. Toast

While Melba is out shakin' her groove thing, her husband, chef Bernie D. Toast, is back in the kitchen cookin' up his world-famous catfish. Melba claims that it was his catfish that caught her heart in the first place back when she was dancin' in Noble, Oklahoma. She says she stopped off at the café he was cookin' at, and after one bite she proposed. Not bein' one to argue with a big gal, he said, yes.

All these recipes that you dive into when you have a meal at The Blue Whale Strip Club have come from Bernie's "recipe box of good food," which he keeps locked up in the club safe. But he's been kind enough to share some of those recipes with me for this book, and I swiped a bunch more out of the safe after he and Melba had fallen asleep durin' that whole quarantine thing. So make sure you check out chef Bernie D. Toast's "good food" items in chapter 6.

Assistant Chef Lucille Dennis

Even though she's fairly new to The Blue Whale Strip Club, many of y'all in the Pangburn area might recognize assistant chef Lucille Dennis if you saw her. She worked for years right alongside High Chaparral Trailer Park resident Ollie White at the Pangburn High School. As a matter of fact, there'd even been talk that once Molly Piper, the gal in charge of the kitchen over there at the school, had retired, Lucille would be the likely choice to take her place. But that all fell through last year for her when a decree came down from up on high that'd flushed her forty-six years of devoted service right down the old toilet. It seemed that someone had decided that smokin' in the kitchen while the lunches were bein' made for the students would no longer be allowed. This basically meant that these poor ladies would have to take their Camels, Lucky Strikes, and Kool Filter Kings outside regardless of what the weather might be like. It also meant that since they'd have to stop what they was doin' in the kitchen to take these smoke breaks, they'd have to get in at four in the mornin' rather than seven if they was gonna get lunch ready by eleven. As you can guess, most of the cafeteria staff wasn't happy with this new policy at all. And since Lucille not only had the senority among the regular staff, but had an exemplary work record that included forty-six years of never missin' a single day of work, she was the one who stood up and told the scholastic hierarchy what the folks in the kitchen thought about this no-smokin'-in-the-kitchen regulation. And for a dramatic effect, she even told 'em that they could either rethink the change in policy or accept her resignation. Lucille seems to enjoy workin' alongside Chef Bernie, and even though he doesn't require her to wear her hairnet unless the health inspector is on property, she says she feels naked without it. So if you find a hair in your food at the Blue Whale, you can bet it ain't Lucille's. A cigarette ash, yes, but a hair, *no way.* Welcome aboard, Lucille!

Our Dishwasher and Food Prep Man

Dang Van Bang

Dang came to us all the way from Vietnam. Bernie and Melba didn't run an ad over there or nothin' like that, Dang was already here in Arkansas. He and his family moved to the U.S. way back durin' the war, and went from California to Oklahoma and finally to Searcy, where six years ago we snagged him and his family. And, boy, did we get lucky. Not only can Dang clean a plate till is shines like the top of most our patrons heads, but his family keeps the Blue Whale lookin' like a show palace. You see, every mornin' after all of us have gone home, Dang's wife, kids, and momma come in and clean the place. And they're real good, too. And I'll tell you what, all of 'em together can't weigh more then 240 pounds wet, but they're still able to lift Little Linda and vacuum under her when they've come in durin' the mornins and found her passed out on the dressin' room floor. I only pray that they wore gloves or used a board to wedge her big bottom up.

Thanks to Dang and his family. They all do a bang-up job.

BEHIND THE BAR

Our Bartender

Billy Merle Pearl

Billy Merle is not only sexy, but at twenty-six he's also the youngest member of the Blue Whale staff. He's been employed here as our bartender for seven years now, and I got to tell y'all that he sure is a pleasure to work with. A lot of normal folks would've just given up on life if they'd lost both their hands in a freak combine accident at the age of sixteen like Billy Merle did. But Billy Merle ain't just like normal folks. Instead of worryin' what others thought about him, he decided that since the good Lord had saved his life, he might as well enjoy it. So after gettin' used to the hooks that'd now be his hands, and gettin' the go from his doctor, Billy Merle went back to play on the high school football team. Let me tell y'all, the folks around here just couldn't get enough of him. As wide receiver, that boy made a touchdown with every ball he caught. And he was somethin' to watch. For some reason, he was always open and no one was ever able to tackle him, well, not since that one poor kid from one of our nothern rival teams tried durin' Billy Merle's first game back, and trust me when I tell y'all that the puncture wound wasn't all that deep. Anyhow, we went on to win the state finals both years that Billy Merle played. And after school and doin' some dead-end jobs, he finally went off to Little Rock and attended the prestigious Razorback Martini College, where after three long weeks of high intensity trainin' he was ready to work in the wonderful world of adult beverages. Since they always have me come down to the college once a month to help out with the class finals (I quiz these kids like there's no tomorrow), I was able to offer Billy Merle the job of head bartender at the club. I did this of course with Melba's blessin'. Well, long story short, he said yes, and you should see that boy behind the bar. Not only can he serve those drinks just like Mr. Tom Cruise in that movie *Cocktail,* but you should see what he can do with flamin' drinks. And I got to tell y'all that I was I impressed with both his natural bartendin' skills, as well as his ability to unhook my bra in less than a second with them steel tools of love.

So make sure to say hi to Billy Merle when you stop by, and, ladies, he's taken by all of us gals at the Blue Whale, so stand back unless you're in the mood for broken-bottle hair coif'.

ON THE DOOR

Our ID checker, bouncer, and cashier

Di Keys

Di has got to be one of the most talented women I know, and I ain't talkin' about strippin'. God bless her, she can fix just about anything from a squeaky door hinge to that 1967 Ford pickup truck of hers with the dual toolboxes and the detachable camper, which she sets up on a stand in the parkin' lot of the R.U. Inn. But, boy howdy, is that gal flat-chested. Oh, let me tell y'all, she could win a dang particleboard look-alike contest hands down. But that's just fine by Di. After all, since she also happens to be the club bouncer, her flat chest is just fine and doesn't get in the way when she has to throw out a few bikers who want to get handsy with one of the gals. But of course, her lack thereof has made for some embarrassin' moments. Like the time we was eatin' at a restaurant in Hebber Springs and the owner tried to drag her out of the women's rest room 'cause he thought she was a man. He was so embarrassed, but with her tiny chest, little mustache, short haircut, and the fact that she wears that tool belt 24/7, it's a common mistake with Di. Why, she can't begin to tell you how many times she's been outside doin' some construction work for Kenny and Donny's antique store or even over here at the Blue Whale when somebody from out of town would pull up and say, "Excuse me, sir, but" followed by some kind of question on how to get somewhere.

Speakin' of extra work, all us folks around here try to find somethin' that Di can fix just so we can give her some money. I feel sorry for her, and I don't know what she does with her money. God bless her, she and her roommate, Lola La Doushe, who also happens to be our cocktail and food waitress, both live in room 13 at the newly opened R.U. Inn (even though I hate the family that owns that, I won't say nothin' about it right here in print on account of me not wantin' to see those hateful cows try to get back at me by throwin' Lola and Di out on the street). I guess their money is so tight for both those gals that they're forced to sleep in the same bed at the motel. And they ain't ones to take charity neither, 'cause I offered to give 'em enough money so they could move up to a room with two beds. Of course they wouldn't have that. And personally, I think that their livin' condition also happens to be why neither one of 'em dates. Sure, men offer, but they both turn 'em down like they would a cold piece of fish. I just wish Di would take one of these guys up on their offers. Lola is attractive, and she'll always have men barkin' on her doorstep, but Di, well, let's just say that you don't find too many men who want to go out with a gal who chews Skoal.

ON THE FLOOR

Our Waitress

Lola La Doushe

In all my years in the business, I got to tell y'all that I ain't never seen a gal who was more talented at both cocktail and food waitressin' than Lola. She's good. And not only can she remember every drink a person orders in that bar, but she can also carry a full tray in each hand and seven or eight more drinks on that chest that the good Lord blessed her with. Why she'd make Dolly Parton cry in a wet T-shirt contest. But she ain't got no desire to dance. She's just happy and content to waitress at the Blue Whale instead. She's one of the most refined southern ladies you'll ever see waitressin' in a bar, but she ain't got nothin' to worry about when it comes to rowdy customers. Why, if a customer so much as looks at her funny, Di, our club bouncer and Lola's roommate, is on that man faster than Little Linda on a Susie Q. So when Lola comes to take your order, keep your hands on the table and don't look her directly in the eye if you know what's good for you.

ON THE RECORD PLAYER

Our DJ

Mildred Brickey

Chain-smokin' Mildred Brickey, at age seventy-six, is still the DJ at the Blue Whale. Now, since the only people that dance are us Blue Whale girls, Mildred ain't your typical DJ, if you know where I'm comin' from. Actually she ain't never had no kind of DJ experience before she landed this job, but she did meet the requirements of the newspaper classified ad that Melba placed. She was able to work weeknights and Saturdays, she didn't mind bein' around cigarette smoke, and she knew how to work an eight-track player as well as an eight-track recorder, which was important since that's what the sound system at the Blue Whale consists of. This really makes it easy in between shows for Mildred, since all she has to do is pop in an eight-track cassette and then she can just go lie down on her cot in the storage room. And once it's close to show time somebody just wakes her up so she can collect our eight-track cassettes with the music on 'em that we girls want to strip to for that show, get her pitcher of vodka stingers and bag of Funyuns, and then take her place in the DJ booth. Mildred is both funny and a joy to work with, although her breath will knock you down. I guess it's on account of the cross between the Funyuns and her five-pack a day smokin' habit, but, boy, that gal can make a dead cow cry after a two-minute conversation. I know for sure she ain't eatin' the mints we keep puttin' in the DJ booth, but I got no idea what the heck she does with 'em.

So the next time you visit The Blue Whale Strip Club and the music stops right in the middle of one of our exotic acts, that deep scratchy voice that's piercin' the dimly lit club, sayin', "Just give it a freakin' minute and the track will change," belongs to none other than our very own DJ Mildred Brickey.

Chapter 1

My newest coworker, Ms. Flora Delight, shows off her personal minibar, back by her dressing table. Not only is she fun to work with, but when the bar ice freezes together, she's always happy to break it up with her wooden leg for all us gals. Welcome aboard, girl!

Types of Home Bars

There is a difference between settin' up a bar at home and the bar you will find in a club. And when it comes to personal bars, there are probably about as many kinds as there are different kinds of drinkers. So in this chapter I'm gonna give you a short description and what's found in the basic bar and several others that seem to be the most popular. I've also included my own personal bar that you'd find if I picked you up off the street and brought you home to my trailer. So pick out a good location in your livin' room, family room, or recreational area, or even your garage, and pick the bar that suits you the best.

BASIC BAR

All the white liquors like rum, vodka, gin, and tequila; dark liquors like bourbon and scotch; liqueurs and cordials; mixers and soft drinks; beer and wine; and garnishes and condiments. Napkins and glassware. Cubed and crushed ice.

BAPTIST BAR

The same as your basic bar only on wheels so if somebody rings your doorbell you can just push it into the closet.

AMATEUR BAR

Orange juice, one white liquor, no garnishes, may or may not contain ice, some kind of stupid corny sign or lamp pertainin' to the art of drinkin'.

EPISCOPALIAN

Fully stocked, loaded, and ready for any planned or unplanned party event or charity social.

DEMOCRAT BAR

When a Republican is in office, heavily stocked and often.

REPUBLICAN BAR

When a Democrat is in office, heavily stocked and often, but with better booze.

WEST COAST BAR

Lots of fruit garnishes, citrus mixers, California wines, and raw fish.

EAST COAST BAR

No mixers, just straight booze—also known as the Kennedy Bar.

NORTHERN BAR

Just like the Basic Bar, but with lots of cheese products.

SOUTHERN BAR

Mostly beer, shooters, and lots of Jell-O. Somethin' stolen from a real bar that usually plugs into the wall and might have cigarette burns. Oh, and don't forget your mint.

TRAILER PARK BAR

Special mixers like Dr Pepper, Orange Crush, Chocolate Soldier, RC Cola, Squirt, and Tab (see chapter 2). Any beer that's on sale or that you got from a beer run, no fruit garnishes, (the only fruit we buy is for cobbler and pies), and shaved ice 'cause it's the only kind the Gas and Smokes sells.

DONNA SUE'S BAR

When it comes to booze you name, I got it, full ashtrays, paper cups or no cups at all, it don't matter, and no garnishes, since food tends to spoil your drunk.

Chapter 2

Our sexy bartender Billy Merle Pearl shows our cocktail/food waitress Lola La
Doushe how his drink-slingin' skills are even better than Tom Cruise's were in
that bartending movie, by mixin' with flamin' alcohol.

Bartendin' Basics

We all know there are a lot of different terms and/or names when it comes to the art of mixology, and leave it to a professional drinker like me to combine 'em all in one chapter. There ain't no reason a drinkin' experience in the comfort of your own trailer home should be any different from the kind you have at your favorite drinkin' establishment, except there's nobody to throw you out or cut you off, especially if you get your partner or mate drunk first. So, here are some of the most common terms, tips, measurements, booze, and a whole cornucopia of other basics you'll need for mixin' up some great drinks.

STOCKIN' YOUR BAR

You'll probably want to buy a selection of liquors and mixers. It's impossible to make a list that'll suit everyone without includin' every possible liquor in the world (I had a hot flash just thinkin' about that), but here's a few guidelines on what to buy. I try to keep a little bit of variety in my trailer but sometimes you just have to say "shut up and drink what I give ya."

Some would say to buy what suits your guests, but I never know until closin' time who may end up at my trailer, if you know what I mean. Since I like just about anythin' that gives me a buzz, I buy a lot of a little bit of everythin'. Young people tend to be wimp drinkers and like the more exotic drinks, so they like all them fruit juices and flavored liqueurs instead of the strong stuff that we professional drinkers prefer. It's likely you'll experience requests for drinks you can't make, which is why you bought this

24

book in the first place, so, dear drinkers, keep it where you can find it, and not just under that broken leg on the couch.

A well-stocked bar should have the followin' hard liquor and wines, but you should consider the number and types of guests you're expectin' to entertain before buyin' a bunch of stuff you don't need. Just remember it's better to have too much of one type of liquor than not to have enough. You don't want an unhappy guest to tip over your trailer 'cause you ran out of sweet vermouth.

- Beer (whatever is on sale)
- Bourbon
- Canadian whiskey
- Cognac (or other brandy)
- Gin
- Rum (light and dark)
- Scotch whiskey
- Tequila (light or gold)
- Vermouth (dry and sweet)
- Vodka
- Wine (red, white, and blush)

Cordials and Liqueurs

Here are some different liqueurs and cordials you might want to have on hand to make some of the drinks in this book. Now, don't go thinkin' you have to have all these things in your bar. Just buy what you want to drink or mix that night (or day). You'd have to have a bunch of money to have all these fixin's in your bar. The ones with the check marks are the ones that you'll use the most.

√ Amaretto (almond)
  Anisette (anise)
  Benedictine (herbs)
  Chambord (black raspberry)

Chartreuse (herbs)

Cointreau (orange, like curaçao)

√ Crème de cacao (light and dark)

Crème de cassis (black currant)

√ Crème de menthe (light and green)

Crème de violette (lavender)

√ Curaçao (orange)

Frangelico (hazelnut) or hazelnut liqueur

√ Galliano (herbs and spices)

√ Godiva (chocolate) Whoa, boy, is it ever chocolate!

√ Goldschläger (cinnamon, flecked with gold leaf bits)

√ Grand Marnier (champagne and orange curaçao)

√ Irish cream (whiskey and cream)

Kahlúa (coffee)

Mandarine Napoleon (tangerine)

Midori (melon) or melon liqueur

√ Ouzo (anise)

√ Peter Heering (cherry)

Sambuca (wild elderberries)

√ Schnapps (variety of flavors, peach, peppermint, apple, butterscotch, etc.)

√ Southern Comfort (peach)

√ Tia Maria (coffee)

Triple sec (orange, like curaçao)

Mixers and Supplies

In addition to the liquors, you will need different mixers, flavorin's, and garnishes. The brands I suggest are available at Lamb's Super Store in Pangburn, but if you don't live nearby, feel free to substitute whatever kind you can find in your own area.

- Bitters, orange and regular
- Blender, or detachable boat/trollin' motor
- Club soda—Schweatz Club Soda
- Coconut cream

- Coffee
- Cola
- Cranberry juice
- Dr Zipper—only from Lamb's (or Dr Pepper)
- Ginger ale—Schweatz Ginger Ale
- Grapefruit juice
- Grenadine
- Heavy cream
- Lemon juice
- Lemon-lime sodas such as Spite
- Lime juice (fresh and sweetened)
- Milk
- Orange juice
- Pineapple juice
- RC Cola, if you have a lot of money
- Shaker glass, plastic cup with a lid, or Tupperware product
- Strainer or knee-high hose
- Sweet 'n' sour mix, juices, sodas, tonics, or waters, if you must
- Tomato juice
- Tonic water—Schweatz Tonic Water
- Worcestershire sauce

Condiments

You should always have a few necessities for flavorin' your drinks. Just like you season your food, some drinks need some added flavor, spice, or sweetness—or so say some folks.

- Bitters (regular and orange)
- Grenadine
- Ground black pepper
- Ground cinnamon
- Nutmeg (grated)
- Salt
- Sugar syrup (aka simple syrup)

- Superfine sugar
- Tabasco sauce

Garnishes (if you're feelin' rich and fancy)

- Celery
- Cocktail onions or any garden-variety onion (Note: Red onions will change the color of your drink.)
- Green olives (small)
- Lemons
- Limes
- Maraschino cherries
- Oranges
- Pineapple

Now, I sometimes garnish my drinks with those little airline bottles of liquor to make 'em a little stronger. I also like soakin' my fruit in liquor the night before a party to give it a little added *flavor*.

Equipment

When settin' up your bar you gotta have the right equipment. So here is a list of the basic bar equipment you should have to make about any kind of refreshment.

- Bottle opener
- Chair for needin' to sit down while you make your drinks as the night goes on.
- Cocktail napkins, paper towels, or those ones you shove by the handfuls in your purse from McDonald's
- Corkscrew for your wines
- Different sizes of spoons
- Dishes for your garnishes
- Electric blender if you want to make frozen concoctions
- Funnel

- Ice, both plain and fancified
- Ice bucket or ice chest
- Ice scoop
- Jigger or shot glass for measurin'
- Juice squeezer
- Knife and cuttin' board
- Plate for salt and sugar
- Straws and stirrers
- Toothpicks for your garnishes
- Vegetable peeler

Glassware

Below you'll find all the common barware that you'll need. Since some of y'all won't have access or the cash to buy these glasses, I've included substitutes that work just fine.

- Highball glass or Cheese Whiz jar, about 10 to 12 ounces
- Rocks glass or a small instant coffee jar, about 6 to 8 ounces
- Collins glass or tall skinny olive jar, about 10 to 12 ounces
- Martini, champagne, or cocktail glass, or a votive candleholder on a stick, about 4 to 6 ounces
- Shooter, NyQuil cup, or ketchup cup from McDonald's, about 1 to 1½ ounces
- Wine glass or jelly jar, about 6 to 8 ounces (thin for white and fat for red)
- Brandy snifter or small fish bowl without the fish, rocks, and plastic plants, about 8 ounces
- Hurricane glass or Miracle Whip jar, about 20 to 24 ounces
- Margarita glass or a large plugged-up funnel on a candlestick, whatever size you can find, 6 to 8 ounces
- Beer glass or mug (why you need a glass for this I don't know), the bigger the better
- Cordial glass or plastic film canister, about 1½ ounces
- Sherry glass or medicine bottle, about 2 to 3 ounces

Measurements

Both the conventional chart and the nonconventional list that follows it will help to ensure that you make each drink the same. Just remember, if you're ever makin' a drink for me, whatever's on the chart, triple it.

Conventional

1 dash/splash	=	$\frac{1}{32}$ ounce
1 teaspoon	=	$\frac{1}{8}$ ounce
1 tablespoon	=	$\frac{3}{8}$ ounce
1 pony	=	1 ounce
1 jigger	=	1 $\frac{1}{2}$ ounces
1 shot	=	1 $\frac{1}{2}$ ounces
1 wineglass	=	4 ounces
1 split	=	6 ounces
1 cup	=	8 ounces
$\frac{1}{2}$ pint	=	8 ounces or 200 ml
1 pint	=	16 ounces or 500 ml
1 quart	=	32 ounces or 1,000 ml
$\frac{1}{2}$ gallon	=	64 ounces or 1,750 ml
1 fifth	=	25.6 ounces or 750 ml
1 gallon	=	128 ounces

Nonconventional

Dash—same as a pinch, splash, or smidge

Fifth—smaller than a quart (We don't mess with fifths unless we *have* to measure. We prefer goin' with quarts and half gallons.)

Jigger—about an ounce and a half

Jug—usually a gallon milk jug

Mouthful—dependin' on your mouth, usually about 2 to 4 ounces

Pinch—same as a dash, splash, or smidge

Smidge—same as a dash, splash, or pinch

Splash—same as a dash, pinch, or smidge

Split—pour half your drink in another cup for a friend

Three Fingers—depends on how big around your glass is, 3 to 10 ounces
Two Fingers—depends on how big around your glass is, 2 to 6 ounces

WAYS TO MIX A DRINK

Blendin' You should use an electric blender to mix ingredients that do not blend easily in any other way. Blend the cocktail till it has reached a smooth consistency or has a foamy head on top. If you are makin' frozen drinks, put the liquor and mixes in first, then add ice till you have the same amount of ice as you have liquid. Crushed ice works best and is easier on your blender. Blend just until you don't see any large chunks. Blendin' too long will make your drink thin and watery.

Helpful hint: Put the lid on the blender *before* you turn it on.

Layerin' Sometimes you may want one liquor to sit on top of another and not mix, to make a layered effect. What you want to do is hold a drinkin' straw or your spoon upside down against the side of your glass. Then pour your liquor over it real slow and let it trickle down the side. I usually ain't got time for this kinda thing. But I say whatever blows your skirt up, honey.

Helpful hint: If usin' a straw, don't try to suck at the same time you're tryin' to layer.

Muddlin' Now, contrary to what Little Linda will tell you, muddlin' is not a combination of four wheelin' and mud wrestlin'. But there are times when you want to dissolve sugar in some fruit juice so it melts and ain't gritty like sand, or you might want to bring out the flavor of some fruit or mint. You do this by puttin' it in the bottom of a rocks glass and carefully mashin' it around with the back of a spoon for a minute or two. You get more flavor out of the fresh ingredients.

Helpful hint: Don't try to do this with a plastic spoon unless you're wearin' safety goggles, 'cause it will break on you and make you mad. You should use a wooden spoon or an ice tea spoon.

Shakin' If you want to serve a drink cold and without ice you would put ice in your shaker and then all the ingredients. Put the lid on and shake for about a minute. Then take the lid off, put on your strainer, and strain your drink into a chilled glass.

Now, if you just want to mix your liquor and pour it over ice (so it doesn't get so diluted), just pour all your ingredients into the shaker and shake a couple of seconds. Then pour the drink over ice.

Helpful hint: Make sure your shaker has a lid or a glass that fits tight down it it; you don't want your drink all over the ceiling.

Stirrin' To mix a drink, stir it with a spoon or straw in a mixin' glass. You should stir only a few times to properly mix a drink. Excess stirrin' will cause the ice to dilute a drink.

Helpful hint: Make sure to lick the spoon or straw so as not to waste any good liquor.

GENERAL DRINK RECIPES

This is a list of the basic classic drink families that tend to be very common in the world of drink mixin'. The drinks have a two-word name with the first name typically comin' from the liquor you put in it. The second word or name comes from the drink family. An example of this would be a Brandy Alexander. But sometimes you'll find that the first name comes from out of nowhere even though the last name comes from the basic drink family, such as a Tom Collins, which is made with gin. But this doesn't need to be as confusin' as it sounds. All you need to remember is a recipe for each drink family and you can add whatever liquor the drinker might want. Now there are many variations of the first names but if you know how a type of drink is basically made and measured you should be able to make about anythin'. With that said, it's time to meet our families!

ALEXANDER

2 ounces liquor or liqueur
2 ounces white or dark crème de cacao
2 ounces light cream

Shake and strain into a highball glass.

COLLINS

1½ ounces liquor
3 ounces sour mix or 3 ounces fresh lime juice plus 1 teaspoon
    powdered sugar
Splash of club soda or 7UP

Shake the first two ingredients, strain into a collins glass of ice, and top with club soda or 7UP.

COOLER

1½ ounces liquor
Ginger ale, 7UP, or Club Soda

Put the liquor into highball glass or wineglass with ice, then top it off with ginger ale or club soda.

FRUIT DAIQUIRI

1 part light rum
1 part sour mix or fresh lime juice

2 parts fresh fruit
Sugar to taste

Blend all the ingredients and serve in an exotic glass with a straw or in a mason jar (like you'd have an exotic glass).

GIMLET

2 ounces liquor
½ ounce Rose's Lime Juice

Put into a lowball or rocks glass with ice, or shake with ice and strain into a martini or cocktail glass.

HIGHBALL

1½ ounces liquor
Water, club soda, or your favorite soda pop

Put the liquor into a highball glass with ice, then top it off with water, club soda, or soda pop.

RICKEY

1 ½ ounces liquor
Club soda
Lime wedge for garnish

Put the liquor into a highball glass over ice, fill it up with club soda, and garnish with the lime wedge.

SLING

1½ ounces liquor
3 ounces sour mix

1 ounce club soda
Maraschino cherry for garnish
Orange slice for garnish

Shake the first two ingredients together, strain into a collins glass filled with ice, and top with the club soda. Garnish with the cherry and orange slice.

SOUR

1½ ounces liquor
3 ounces sour mix
Maraschino cherry for garnish
Orange slice for garnish

Shake the first two ingredients together, then strain into a lowball glass filled with ice or serve straight up without ice in a chilled sour glass. Garnish with the cherry and orange slice.

SPRITZER

1½ ounces liquor
Club soda

Put the liquor into a highball glass with ice and top it off with club soda.

STINGER

1½ ounces crème de menthe
1½ ounces liquor

Shake with ice and strain into a chilled cocktail or martini glass or serve on the rocks in a lowball glass.

TIPS

Here are some tips that will help you to create some perfect drinks. They sure have come in handy for me and my fellow Blue Whale gals. By the way, if you're a man, you might want to memorize these, 'cause if I pick you up after a show there will be a test first before you touch my trailer bar.

- Another method of garnishin' is to delicately wipe juice around the rim of a glass and dip the top of the glass into a garnish such as salt for Margaritas, sugar for Daiquiris, or cocoa powder for Chocolate Martinis. This is known as "rimmin'." Just make sure that when you do this little job on your glass that you get plenty of the garnish on the rim. If not, then the drink doesn't taste right. And trust me on this one, there ain't nothin' worse than gettin' a bad rim job. So make your guests happy, and rim 'em good.

- When makin' cocktails, don't be afraid of tastin' a guest's drink before servin' it since some delicately balanced drinks require that you check to make sure you got it just right. You do this by placin' a straw in the drink, puttin' your finger over the top of the straw, and then pullin' it out with that finger still in place. Then bring the straw to your mouth and take your finger off the hole. If you want to get a real good taste, you always got to take your finger off the hole. But never ever take a sip from a guest's glass, unless you know for sure he's in the bathroom or you duck under the bar first.

- Here's a tip if you ever have to tend bar anywhere. Never put glassware of any sort in your ice well, as a small chip from a glass is invisible to the keenest eye but could easily cut a customer's mouth and ruin any chance of gettin' a decent tip. Well, I guess if a customer's mouth is bloody you ain't gettin' a tip anyways unless you can manage to get his wallet while you help the paramedics lift him up onto the stretcher!

- Put your glasses in the freezer when you can—especially martini and beer glasses. This makes your drinks stay cold longer. If you have no freezer space available, add ice and soda water to the glass before makin' the drink to chill the glass down, or put them in one of those 99¢ Styrofoam coolers from the local Taco Tackle Shack or Lamb's Super Store.

Tupperware and plastic glasses, like you get from Gas and Smokes, don't freeze or keep your drink very cold.

- When makin' your drinks, you need to always fill the glass with ice; this does not mean that you'll get any less alcohol or that the drink will be diluted quicker. In fact, the drink will water down a lot slower; a lot of ice will keep the drink cold longer, which keeps the ice from meltin'. You don't want watered-down drinks, but if you are like me and girls at the Blue Whale you don't keep a drink long enough for the ice to even start meltin'. So if you're makin' me a drink, skip the ice unless I ask for it.

- Remember the bar is a stage and you are the star. Your surroundin's add atmosphere and quality drinks taste great, but it's you that makes it all work. Of course, if I happen to be in that same room, your show is over—so just pour the dang drinks, and make mine a double.

Chapter 3

Durin' Ladies' Night at the Blue Whale, cashier and bouncer Di Keys enjoys her favorite drink of choice, beer, while she goes over the tips for mouth-to-mouth resuscitation in case of an emergency.

Beer

Even though beer ain't my favorite drink, mind you, I ain't never turned one down, I was surprised at the recent discovery by archaeologists that before humankind learned how to make bread, they'd already been brewin' beer. Actually, *surprised* is the wrong word. *Relieved* is more along the lines of what I was thinkin'. I was relieved on account of now when Sister Bertha or one of her uppity group tries to preach about the evils of a bottle of beer, I can turn around and give 'em the "what's what." And I got to tell you, folks, I have a hard time believin' that the good Lord's got a problem with beer. Now, before some of y'all faint away, let me make my point. In Sunday school back when I was a little girl, we was taught that God's chosen people was the Israelites. He kept his hands on 'em, guided 'em, and even showed 'em where and how to live. And we was told that the Bible was the word of God. Well, if that's the case, then why does the Good Book say that his chosen people named a location in the Holy Land Beersheba? With the way Sister Bertha talks, it should have been called Watersheba or Sweet Teasheba. Say what you want about my theory, but let me just give you two more things to think about that I also learned in Sunday school. If you go to 1 Kings 19:3, you'll find out that Elijah ran to Beersheba when the wicked Jezebel ordered him killed. Now you tell me, how many times has this happened? Why I've known many a man run to beer on account of some wicked Jezebel. And last but not least, we've all heard the story of Jacob seein' the angels walkin' up that ladder, right? Well, did you know that accordin' to Genesis 28:10 that happened in Beersheba, which goes right along with my point that if you give a man a few beers, everybody looks like an angel. So I'm thinkin' we need to get some theologians on this one before we actually put down our mug, can, or bottle, if you know what I mean.

Them archaeologists that I mentioned earlier got 'emselves a 3,800-year-old clay tablet showin' that in 1720 B.C., durin' the time that King Hammurabi (I think Ila LaFleur dated his cousin) reigned in Mesopotamia, beer was drunk by all members of society includin' women, so stick that in your Sunday hat, Sister Bertha, and wear it. They even believe that the earliest cereal to be farmed was barley, which was growin' wild. And since it was hard to knead into bread, they simply mixed it with water and fruit, and when it fermented, it turned into a light alcoholic drink. But of course, we folks in the trailer parks and rural communities across the country have always known beer was good for you.

Regardless if we drink it in public with it comin' straight out of the bar fridge or in private from the portable cooler we keep under the bed, beer has always played an important part in our lives. For example, how many of y'all can say that your parents met while enjoyin' a tall cold one? Yes, every night of the year all across this planet of ours, folks are startin' up conversation with a person that they've noticed from across the room while poppin' a top or twistin' a cap. And let me tell y'all that to be honest, even though it was the beer that gave 'em the courage to walk up to that person in the first place, it most certainly did absolutely nothin' to inspire their originality or use of the English language. The pickup lines are still terrible, and I ought to know, 'cause I've personally heard and used 'em all from time to time. With that in mind, and since we all know you're goin' out this weekend, or, for those of you who are already with somebody you love, if you're in the mood for a little hanky-panky this month, I've decided to help y'all out by includin' some of the best lines that have either entered my ears or exited my hole. And with these openin' phrases, if they're delivered right close to closin' time, you're sure to reel one in. Now these won't work for everyone. If you're as ugly as sin or Opal Lamb-Inman who runs Lamb's Super Store, then your best bet for pickin' up somebody is to just to stop by the bank, get a couple of hundred-dollar bills, and right about 1:30 A.M., tape those suckers to your forehead, and stand in a dark section of the bar. But for everyone else, keep readin' and start memorizin'.

1. You know my granny wears that same perfume you got on.
2. I bet you've never slept with a man with thirteen toes before?
3. You look like a woman with class, but hopefully not tonight.
4. It looks like God used the good spit when he made you.
5. I bet you've never had sex while two coon dogs licked your feet, have you?
6. Excuse me, but your hairpiece is on fire.
7. Ouch! My tooth hurts! . . . Because you are sooo sweet!
8. Hey, hon, if that good-lookin' friend of yours don't change her mind before I leave, would you like to come home with me instead?
9. You know you can get them bras that'll push all that up, don't you?
10. Why if you ain't the prettiest thing I've ever laid eyes on, may the Lord make my rash spread to places I can't see.
11. Didn't I see you last Tuesday comin' out of the free clinic around two-thirty in the afternoon?
12. Have you ever slept with a man that was wanted for murder?
13. When you turn your head just right, that mole ain't so bad lookin'.
14. Excuse me, but you didn't happen to do time with my sister, did you?
15. You sure are one good looker from the neck down.
16. So is that a Tootsie Roll in your pocket or are you just happy to see me?
17. Forgive me if this sounds forward, but I just wanted you to know that I got a pillow at home callin' your name, and a blanket that your dog can sleep on in the livin' room.
18. Have you ever wondered what your aunt would look like naked?
19. You're prettier than a beer truck pullin' up in my driveway!
20. I love women who aren't afraid to put on a few pounds.

Now when it comes to beer there is more than just Coors, Bud, and Miller. There are thousands of breweries right here in the good old US of A, and plenty in other countries, too. Beer has been made for thousands of years. Here are the basics types and some interestin' facts you might want to know.

- One of the things Noah brought on the ark was beer. Two cans, two bottles, and two kegs. Go forth and multiply!
- Beer was once valued so highly that workers were paid with it. I've been known to take a few bottles as payment myself.
- Egyptians brewed beer for royalty and medical purposes, and even buried people with it to take with them to the afterlife. This reminds me of the time Little Linda got wasted on Pabst Blue Ribbon and tried to bury me. Luckily she passed out before she got my face completely covered.
- They have found medical prescriptions callin' for beer by the Egyptians as far back as 1600 B.C. I always knew there was a good reason for drinkin'.
- If an Egyptian man offered a lady some of his beer they were engaged. I don't know if I like that custom or not.
- Even monasteries and convents used to make beer. I think the Lutherans have since taken over this practice.
- Queen Elizabeth I drank beer for breakfast. Atta girl!
- The first beer brewed in this country was at Sir Walter Raleigh's colony in Virginia. I think that was the colony that disappeared.
- Now, they don't teach this in school, but in 1620 the Pilgrims landed at Plymouth Rock because the beer supplies were gettin' low. In honor of this I always make sure to drink beer with my Thanksgivin' meals. One tall boy for every ounce of turkey.
- George Washington loved beer and wrote his own recipe. He, Thomas Jefferson, and William Penn, all owned their own breweries. God Bless America!
- Durin' the Revolutionary War, the soldiers each got a quart of beer a day. Now you know why they called 'em minutemen.
- The same fellow who discovered penicillin also started pasteurizin' beer years before people pasteurized milk. I've found that penicillin and beer do go hand in hand.
- Teddy Roosevelt took about five hundred gallons of beer with him on a huntin' safari in Africa. That's nothin': I keep five hundred gallons of beer in the trunk of my Bonneville any given Saturday night.
- In 1935 the first beer can was introduced. Yes, they're more convenient but it's hard to break 'em open durin' a bar fight.

- In 1966 Budweiser was the first brand to sell ten million barrels in a year. Flossy LaFleur swears she bought half of that.
- Beer should be drunk within three to four months of the time it is made. Not a problem.

There are a just few types of beer but a million ways to brew it, store it, and age it. It's gettin' to be as complicated as wine. I'll tell you what the basics mean, but after that it's up to you to go out and try 'em until you find the ones you like.

Ales Fruitier flavor that comes from a quicker and hotter fermentation process. This is the oldest beer style in the world and is produced by warm or top fermentation.

Bock Beers Usually heavy, strong lagers with a high alcohol content and malt flavor, mainly from Germany. These are so heavy that drinkin' 'em is like eatin' dinner. I love the Germans!

Dry Less sweet with little or no aftertaste. I don't think it has any taste at all, but that's just my opinion.

Lager Smooth and light beer with a slightly tangy taste. These are real good and a glass of lager reminds me of big sweaty men cuttin' trees.

Light One third or one half the amount of alcohol and calories in ordinary beer. You may like these if you're watchin' your figure or not wantin' to get drunk. I say, "WHY BOTHER?"

Malts Lager beers with a higher amount of alcohol than pilsners. Now we're talkin' my kind of beer!

Pale Ale Light, slightly fruity ale. Don't ask me to explain that one 'cause it don't taste like fruit to me.

Pilsner The international brand name for light-colored lager beers, which is mostly what we drink today. Most often the most popular beers in America are pilsners but they may not say it on the label.

Stout At one time an English term for the strongest or "stoutest" beer in a brewery. I not only like this one, but I even like the sound of the name. Who doesn't want somethin' stout? I've even been called stout before when shoppin' for clothes.

Chapter 4

After this experience, I was never able to look at a poor caged bird the same. I still hate that cow Faye Faye LaRue. Oh well, at least, as you can see from this newspaper photo, I made the headlines the following day.

Bourbon / Whiskey

If you all read my sister's foreword, you already know about my beginin's and how I gave up my goals of bein' a nurse to pursue my real dream of bein' an exotic dancer. When I think of whiskey, it brings back a very old memory of when I first started out in the entertainment field. The glamour of the stage was callin' my name, but there were no dancin' clubs in Pangburn, so I knew I would have to expand my search in order to realize my dream. I read in the *Arkansas Gazette* about auditions over in Little Rock for a national go-go dancin' stripper tour. My good friend at the time, Faye Faye LaRue, agreed to go with me, 'cause she wanted to audition too—besides, she had a car. We were out to prove that two big voluptuous girls from a small town in Arkansas could make it big in the stripper world. We were gonna be the Gypsy Rose Lees of Pangburn.

We packed everythin' into Faye Faye's 1960 Nash Rambler and headed to the capital city. We checked on some motels when we got there but decided that ten dollars was just too high for a room and that our money could be better spent on somethin' more important, like food and liquor, so we just decided to sleep in the car and change at the truck stop for the audition. We got the key to the ladies' room and started to get ourselves ready. I put on a mini skirt that stretched so tight around my thighs that you could see the outline of the happy face tattoo on my left bun. Our family didn't have much money, so I couldn't afford them fancy patent leather go-go boots. Instead, I went to a thrift store and got me a pair of combat boots and spray-painted them white, then pinned white fabric around my legs clear up to my thighs. I jacked my hair up as high as my arms would reach and applied my makeup, a generous amount of eye shadow, and frosted lipstick, just like Ruby had taught me, which she had

46

learned from watchin' *American Bandstand*. I haven't changed my style since (as we always say, if somethin' ain't broke, don't fix it).

We were ready and nervous, so we stopped off at a liquor store to pick up somethin' to steady our nerves. We picked up some Crown Royal Blended Whiskey cause Faye Faye said it was real smooth and mixed well with Coke. After gettin' our nerves under control, we headed to the audition at the G-Strings-A-Go-Go club over in south Little Rock.

Lots of girls showed up that day, tall, short, skinny, and us. Momma always said don't talk bad about people, but I tell you some of these girls were so ugly. I remember one in particular that could have played Norman Bates's momma in *Psycho*. I figured the real ugly ones would be cut from the competition first and I was right. After the first song more than half of the girls were out, but Faye Faye and me were still in the runnin'.

Next to go was the tall Amazon-like women. I guess all that marryin' your own cousins made for a lot of seven-foot tall girls in Arkansas back in those days. So all the tall girls were out. Besides they wouldn't fit in the cages.

Next we had to take turns gettin' into the cages and dancin' up in the air. We all drew numbers and as luck would have it Faye Faye and me got the first two. Well, we climbed into our cages and began to get hoisted up into the air like a flyin' circus act. The boys that were doin' the pullin' on the ropes were such weaklin's that it took a dozen of 'em to get us up there above the dance floor.

When the music started and we started go-go dancin', Faye Faye and I were puttin' the other little skinny girls to shame. We had moves we hadn't begun to use yet. Someone put a dime in the jukebox and we began to dance to Diana Ross and the Supremes "Itchin' in My heart." I began to shake and boogie and so did Faye Faye. I was matchin' her every move and we did everythin' from the jerk to the pony. We were friends, but both of us wanted this job, and friendship was not gonna' stand in my way of becomin' a big star on the stripper circuit. Nothin' could deprive me from pleasurin' my audience with my dancin', not to mention the free drinks that came with it.

The next song came blarin' from the jukebox and it was Martha and the Vandellas' "Heat Wave." By now I was hittin' my groove. My Crown Royal was really kickin' in (along with the pint I finished in the ladies' room). Then came the best song of all and my personal favorite, Junior Walker and the Allstars' "Shotgun." Well, this song drove me as wild as a monkey rubbin' his butt in poison ivy. I rocked that cage like Me-Ma does in her rockin' chair when her Ex-Lax is about to kick in. I was doin the jerk so hard that my cage started to rock, and, before long, it was swayin' like a flyin' trapeze.

Faye Faye was givin' it her all, but the girl was sweatin' like a pig in a bacon factory. Her face was as red as a radish and she looked like she was about to pass out. I just had a feelin' if I could just keep up this pace I would win this audition and have the job. I was wavin' to her and smilin' so big I thought my ears would get wet, but deep inside I really wanted her to puke all over the dance floor below. Well, do you know what you get for wishin' evil on someone else? It comes back to bite you in the butt.

I had that cage swingin' so wide that little did I know my rope had been rubbin' on the metal wheel above my head. The friction from my dancin' and swayin' back and forth had cut the rope down to a thread. Faye Faye saw this and hollered "Put in another dime, and play O-69." It was Elvis's "Jailhouse Rock." She knew my rope would never hold out through "I went to a party in the county jail," much less the whole thing. I was doomed. I was wonderin' why she had the smug look on her big round face with the one big eyebrow.

My rope snapped and my cage came crashin' down. I saw sparks and dust and heard the sounds of screechin' metal. I guess when I fell I must have blacked out but they told me I bounced off a row of beanbag chairs and bowled over all the other girls competin'. When I woke up there were seventeen ambulances carryin' off all the girls and Faye Faye and me were the only ones not injured. I think this was largely due to my bein' limber from the Crown Royal and all that dancin'. I didn't have a scratch on me, but I had a huge headache but that could've been fixed if I could find my purse with the rest of that Crown Royal in it.

The owner said he was glad it didn't happen on a busy Saturday when the club was full, and he was thinkin' about puttin' in a giant fountain with a wishin' well in the hole I'd made when I hit the floor. He said since Faye Faye and me were the only two left from the audition we got the jobs (if I promised not to sue and he cut me in for 25 percent of the change the wishin' well brought in for life. A deal that has made Beaver Liquors and me very happy for years. He also said he would put the cages on steel cable instead of rope in the future). We were so excited we went that night and bought some more Crown Royal to celebrate. We even splurged and checked into that $10-a-night motel.

We worked at that club for about a month, polishin' our acts and gettin' our stripper costumes made, before goin' on the stripper circuit with the "professionals." I knew from then on I would have to keep my eye on Faye Faye 'cause she was sneaky.

For the next several years, she would steal my men and my clothes, but, God help her, she knew better than to steal my whiskey. Now I am told, although I don't remember much about it, that the dance "the funky chicken" was conceived by me the night Faye Faye put itchin' powder in my G-string. Don't worry, I have gotten even a few times. But I have never forgivin' her for tryin' to sabotage me at that audition, and she has never forgiven me for puttin' Visine in her drink and givin' her the runs the first night on tour with the professional stripper circuit.

Whiskey has played a large role in the history of our country, believe it or not. I remember readin' in school about the uprisin' known as the "Whiskey Rebellion," which all came about on account of a liquor sin tax. Me-Ma told me at one time or another that her great-great-great-great-great-grandpappy was in it, and for all we know, he may have started it! (Of course she also once told me that if I put cotton in my ears, closed my mouth, and held my breath, when I passed gas I'd fly off like an illegal bottle rocket on the Fourth of July.) Anyhow, sometime in the late eighteenth century, American farmers who made whiskey got dang tired of payin' the huge taxes the government was puttin' on their product. The government told 'em that the taxes was bein' enforced to stop the excessive drinkin' that was goin' on in our country—like that could actually be done. Now, if you've ever lived in the South, then you know you've got about as much luck tellin' us the amount of booze we can drink as you've got gettin' a citizen in the state of Florida to work a votin' machine. Well, the leader of our great country at the time, President George Washington, marched into Pennsylvania leadin' an army to stop the rebellion that the farmers was throwin', and in the end only two people were actually arrested, and they were later pardoned by President Washington. How much you want to bet they was kin to Little Linda?

Now in order to figure out the difference between scotch whisky, better known to you and me as Johnnie Walker, Chivas, or whatever's the cheapest-on-the-shelf scotch, and the American/Irish whiskey like Wild Turkey, Jim Beam, or plain old bourbon, is that the scotch from Scotland ain't got an *e* and the latter does in the spellin' of the word *whiskey*. The other difference is the way it's made. Of course both will still make you sleep with anything breathin' on a cold lonely night, but they do taste different on account of what goes in 'em. There you go, now you know the basic difference between the two. But wait just a minute, 'cause just when you think you got it figured out, our friends to the north, and I ain't talkin' about Iowa, come up with their own "cog in the wheel." That's right, those bacon-eatin', moose-chasin' fools have come up with their own version of the American/Irish whiskey bourbon, better know as Canadian whiskey, and let me tell y'all that if you ever want to make Momma happy, get her a bottle of this stuff and a semiattractive Mountie to share it with. This type of whiskey is so good that brands like Crown Royal, Canadian Mist, and Seagram's 7 have become some of the best-sellin' whiskeys (with an *e*) in the world.

With that all cleared up, let me add just one more thing. There are several different ingredients that can be used in the makin' of whiskeys, such as malt, barley, corn, wheat, rye, and/or all of 'em blended together. Each is mighty good and as different tastin' to a whiskey drinker as say a RC Cola, Dr Pepper, and Mountain Dew is to a Baptist at a church social. Another interestin' fact is that Uncle Sam says that bourbon has to have 51 percent corn, and be aged in brand-new burnt oak barrels for four dog-gone years, if it's to be called bourbon whiskey. I tell you, folks, a gal could get thirsty waitin' on a belt out of that barrel, which is why I always keep my own three-day blend on hand in a coffee can under the sink by the Drano.

Before y'all wake me up in the middle of the day, callin' my trailer, wantin' to know what kind of whiskey/bourbon I drink, let me tell you now: whatever they got on hand. I ain't picky, and when it comes to booze, I'm an equal opportunity drinker. But if I had to pick one, it would have to be good old deep-in-the-heart-of-Dixie Tennessee whiskey, which is made by God-fearin' folks with a dream. Jack Daniel's and George Dickel are two major makers or Tennessee-style whiskey, and I love 'em like family. Their whiskey-makin' process is called sour mash, and if you've ever made that friendship cake or sourdough bread where you take the yeast from the previous batch to start up the new cake or bread dough, then you kind of know how the sour mash process works. They simply take some of the old yeast from the previous batch of whiskey to create the new batch, and just continue borrowin' from each batch thereafter. So the glass of Tennessee whiskey that you're holdin' in your hands actually has DNA particles that can be traced back to the very first batch that plant ever made, unless they spilled it between then and now.

Here are a few of my favorite whiskey drinks.

AMARETTO SNEAKY SOUR

1 ounce whiskey
1 ounce amaretto
1 ounce sour mix

Mix and pour into highball glasses.

ARKANSAS COOLER

1½ ounces blended whiskey
½ ounce cherry-flavored brandy
1 ounce cranberry juice

Shake with ice and strain into a highball glass half filled with ice.

BLUE GRASS COCKTAIL

2 ounces bourbon
1 ounce pineapple juice
1 ounce fresh lemon juice
1 teaspoon maraschino liqueur

Shake with ice and strain into a chilled cocktail glass.

BOURBON PEACH COBBLER

2½ ounces bourbon
1 ounce peach schnapps
1 tablespoon lemon juice
¾ ounce grapefruit juice
1¼ teaspoons almond extract
Ground cinnamon for garnish

Mix the liquid ingredients in a mixin' jar, pour into a glass over ice, and sprinkle cinnamon on top.

BULL AND BEAR

1½ ounces bourbon
¾ ounce orange curaçao
Juice of ½ lime
1 tablespoon grenadine
Orange slice for garnish
Maraschino cherry for garnish

Shake with ice and strain into a cocktail glass. Garnish with the orange slice and cherry.

CALIFORNIA LEMONADE

2 ounces blended whiskey
1½ tablespoons powdered sugar
½ teaspoon grenadine
Juice of 1 lemon
Juice of 1 lime
Club soda
Maraschino cherry for garnish

Shake the first five ingredients with ice and strain into a highball glass filled with shaved ice. Fill with club soda and top with the cherry.

CANADIAN BREEZE

1½ ounces Canadian whiskey
½ teaspoon maraschino
1 teaspoon pineapple juice
1 tablespoon fresh lemon juice
Maraschino cherry for garnish

Shake with ice and strain into a glass half full of ice cubes. Top with the cherry.

CANADIAN SUNSET

1½ ounces Canadian whiskey
1 teaspoon pineapple juice
1 tablespoon lemon juice
½ teaspoon maraschino
Maraschino cherry for garnish

Shake the first three ingredients with ice and strain into a highball glass half full of ice cubes. Top with the maraschino liqueur and cherry.

DAISY DUKE

1½ ounces bourbon
1½ teaspoons lemon juice
1½ teaspoons Simple Syrup (page 148)
5 drops triple sec
Club soda

Shake the first four ingredients with ice. Strain into a glass. Add the ice and fill with club soda.

DAYTONA THUNDER

½ ounce bourbon
1½ ounces Southern Comfort
½ ounce triple sec
½ ounce peach schnapps
Orange juice
Grapefruit juice

Shake all the liquor with crushed ice and strain into a frosted mug filled with ice. Top with orange and pineapple juice and stir. (Perfect for watchin' the race.)

DIXIE STINGER

3 ounces bourbon
½ ounce white crème de menthe
½ teaspoon Southern Comfort

In a shaker half filled with ice cubes, combine all the ingredients. Shake well. Strain into a cocktail glass.

DRY MANHATTAN

2 ounces blended whiskey
1 ounce dry vermouth
Lemon twist for garnish

Mix the whiskey and vermouth in a mixin' pitcher with ice and stir. Strain into a chilled martini glass. Garnish with the lemon twist. (May also be served on the rocks.)

FACE FIRST

⅓ ounce Jim Beam bourbon
⅓ ounce sloe gin
⅓ ounce rum
Splash of grenadine

Combine all the ingredients in a highball glass with cracked ice and you will go down—face first.

IS THAT A BANANA IN YOUR POCKET?

2 ounces whiskey
1 ounce banana liqueur
2 parts Homemade Sweet 'n' Sour Mix (page 147)
7UP

Fill a collins glass with ice. Add the first three ingredients, mix, and top off the glass with 7UP. Stir and enjoy!

KENTUCKY SNOWSTORM

1½ ounces bourbon
1½ ounces cranberry juice
½ ounce Rose's Lime Juice

½ ounce grenadine

1 teaspoon sugar

Orange or lemon slice for garnish

Shake all the ingredients with ice. Strain into a glass or pour into a glass over cracked ice. Top with the orange or lemon slice.

LOUISVILLE CHILL

1½ ounces bourbon

1 ounce orange juice

1 tablespoon Rose's Lime Juice

1 teaspoon powdered sugar

Orange slice for garnish

Shake all the ingredients with cracked ice and strain into a glass over cracked ice. Top with the orange slice.

LOUISVILLE LADY

1 ounce bourbon

¾ ounce white crème de caçao

¾ ounce light cream

Shake with ice and strain into a cocktail glass.

MANHATTAN

1½ ounces blended whiskey

¾ ounce sweet vermouth

Maraschino cherry for garnish

Stir with ice and strain into a cocktail glass. Top with the cherry.

MILLIONAIRE

2 ounces blended whiskey
½ ounce triple sec
¼ ounce grenadine
1 ounce orange juice

Shake all the ingredients in a shaker with ice cubes and strain into a sour glass.

MINT JULEP

4 sprigs of mint
1 teaspoon powdered sugar
2 teaspoons water
2½ ounces bourbon

In a tall glass, mash the mint leaves, powdered sugar, and water. Fill the glass with crushed ice and add the bourbon.

OLD-FASHIONED

Club soda
Dash of Simple Syrup (page 148)
Several dashes of Angostura bitters
2 ounces bourbon

Mix the club soda, syrup, and bitters in an old-fashioned glass. Add the bourbon and ice cubes, then stir.

PSYCHO WARD

2 ounces blended whiskey
Juice of ½ lemon
¼ ounce grenadine

1 teaspoon powdered sugar
Orange slice for garnish
Maraschino cherry for garnish

Shake the whiskey, lemon juice, grenadine, and powdered sugar with ice and strain into a red-wine glass filled with cracked ice. Top with the orange slice and cherry and serve with a straw.

QUICKIE

1 ounce bourbon
1 ounce white rum
¼ ounce triple sec

Shake with ice and strain into a cocktail glass.

RANCH HAND

3½ ounces Jim Beam bourbon
2 ounces Pepsi-Cola
2 ounces Mountain Dew

Fill a pint jar with ice. Pour in the whiskey. Then add the Pepsi and Mountain Dew and stir.

RED HOT LOVIN'

1 ounce bourbon
½ ounce triple sec
1 ounce lemon juice
Dash of grenadine

Shake with ice and strain into a cocktail or martini glass.

ROYAL FLUSH

1 ounce Crown Royal bourbon
1 ounce peach schnapps
4 ounces cranberry juice
4 ounces orange juice
Splash of soda water

Put the bourbon and peach schnapps in a tumbler and fill with the orange juice, cranberry juice, and soda water.

ROYAL SCANDAL

1 ounce Crown Royal bourbon
½ ounce Southern Comfort
½ ounce amaretto
Splash of Homemade Sweet 'n' Sour Mix (page 147)
Splash of pineapple juice

Add the liquors and mixers to a shaker with ice. Shake and strain into a chilled martini glass.

RUG BURN

1 ounce bourbon
1 ounce amaretto
1 ounce peach schnapps
Splash of 7UP

Mix and serve on ice in a rocks glass.

SOUTHERN BELLE

1 ounce whiskey
¾ ounce bourbon
6 ounces pineapple juice
¾ ounce triple sec
2 ounces orange juice
Splash of grenadine

Combine the first five ingredients in a small pitcher with ice. Top with the grenadine and stir. Makes 2.

SOUTHERN PEACH

1½ ounces bourbon
1 ounce peach schnapps
2 ounces orange juice
2 ounces sour mix
⅛ ounce grenadine

Shake the first four ingredients together and pour into a tall glass over ice. Top with the grenadine.

THOROUGHBRED COOLER

1 ounce bourbon
1 ounce sour mix
1 ounce orange juice
Lemon-lime soda
Dash of grenadine

Pour first three ingredients in a glass over ice. Fill with lemon-lime soda and stir. Add the grenadine on top.

WHISKEY COLLINS (JOHN COLLINS)

1 ounce blended whiskey
2 ounces Homemade Sweet 'n' Sour Mix (page 147)
2 ounces club soda or 7UP
Maraschino cherry for garnish
Orange slice for garnish

Mix in shaker cup and pour into a collins glass over ice. Garnish with the cherry and orange slice.

WHISKEY SLING

2 ounces blended whiskey
2 ounces lemon juice
1 teaspoon superfine sugar
1 ounce water
Lemon twist for garnish

Mix in shaker cup, pour into a highball glass over ice, and garnish with the lemon twist.

WHISKEY SOUR

1 ounce blended whiskey
3 ounces Homemade Sweet 'n' Sour Mix (page 147)
Maraschino cherry for garnish
Orange slice for garnish

Mix in shaker cup and pour into a highball glass over ice. Garnish with the cherry and orange slice.

Chapter 5

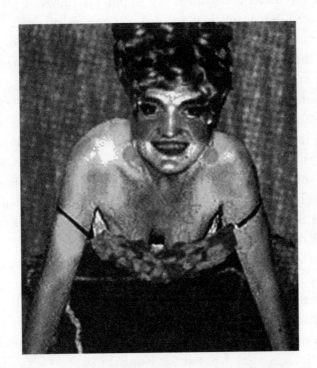

My fellow dancer at the Blue Whale, eighty-four-year-old Ms. Ila "Flossy" LaFleur, can knock back some brandy, but you wouldn't believe how much of that stuff her twenty-two-year-old boyfriend guzzles down just before it's time to close.

Brandies and Cognacs

Have you ever found yourself loungin' in your patio furniture on a beautiful fall evenin' under a star-filled sky sippin' on a lovely glass of brandy? Neither have I, but I can't begin to tell you how many times I've come to in a gutter or under a car with an empty brandy bottle in my hand. But even with that said, brandy ain't my drink of choice. Of course, neither is Old Spice cologne, but I've been known to pour that over a glass of ice with a splash of 7UP on a Sunday when my liquor supply was gone and Beaver Liquors was closed. But trust me when I tell y'all that regardless of how good it might smell, brandy beats Old Spice hands down when it comes to taste.

Speakin' of brandy, I'll never forget the time that my dear friend and fellow Blue Whale Strip Club dancer Flossy, better known around the club by her real name Ila LaFleur, asked me to join her and her twenty-two-year-old boyfriend on a cruise they was takin'. Now before I get any further, I want y'all to understand that Flossy, who happens to be eighty-four, knows that her boyfriend, Digger, is in this relationship simply for the money and the things he can get, which is why she herself will tell y'all that the only reason she keeps it goin' is for the sex. Accordin' to Flossy, she ain't got a lot of money, but she sure is gettin' a lot of sex, which makes me sick to my stomach even as I put those words to paper. Gettin' back to the story, I'd never been on a cruise ship, and Flossy told me that not only would there be single men lookin' for a good time, but once the crew found out who we was, they'd probably want us to perform. With all that, how could I possibly say no. So after packin' a few essentials like my bathin' suit, suntan oil, and fully stocked bar, I was on my way to the wonderful high seas. Or so I thought.

It wasn't until the boat had set sail and I'd asked which island we'd be stoppin' at first that Flossy informed me that our cruise wasn't charted for the beloved Caribbean as I'd assumed, but rather for the cold and white "last frontier" better known as Alaska. I could've killed her! It was freezin' cold once you stepped out on the deck. She kept tellin' me to just enjoy the animals like the moose or whales at play in the wilderness. Yeah, like that lasted for more than five seconds before borin' me to tears. I love animals, but, folks, you got to remember that I dated Vance Poole for a while, and have seen Little Linda skinny-dip. Trust me when I tell y'all that nothin' can top that sight except for nude photos of Mr. Burt Reynolds, and then you got my undivided attention regardless of how dang cold it might be.

And as far as the men go, well, let's just say that Digger won first place for bein' the youngest passenger on the ship, and I came in second. Third place was won by a seventy-three-year-old nun. Listen, some of these folks was so old I got a feelin' they witnessed the first raisin' of the American flag in Alaska back in 1867. I kid you not. I mean some of these folks were so old they'd brought their caskets along. Most of these fellas couldn't lift their hand, let alone anything else, if you know what I mean. By the end of day one I knew I wasn't gonna be gettin' anything out of these "single men," and I let Ila know that I wasn't happy (when I get mad, it's Ila and not Flossy).

When I stopped by Ila's room to tell her how bad my trip was turnin' out to be, she told me to just relax and she had somethin' that would make it a whole lot better. With that she opened up one of her suitcases and pulled out this giant bottle of industrial-strength Viagra. It seems that Digger has to down a few of these before he can perform with Ila, and since all us Blue Whale girls share a dressin' room together, I can't say I blame him. Of course I thanked Ila and had her dump about half of what was in the bottle into my purse. I then went back to my cabin, freshened up a bit, and put on my bikini and walked the inside of the cruise ship.

After the first time around I was a bit disappointed. I'll admit, I ain't no Cindy Crawford, I ain't got a real mole, but you'd have thought someone would have followed me around. Of course I quickly realized that I'd been walkin' too fast for these seniors to catch me. So on the second go-around, I'd slowly walk a few steps, stop for a minute, and then repeat the process.

Well, needless to say, that did it for me. I had so many men hittin' on me that they had to take a number. And to impress me they kept offerin' me things like flowers, candy, and AARP discounts. It was fun, that's for sure. So I finally gave out my cabin number along with one of them special pills to all the men who wanted me, and told 'em to take it before comin' to see me. Well, that was where the fun stopped. I don't know what the deal was with these fellas, but eight out of the twelve guys that I told to come see me showed up with nothin' more than a stiff neck or leg, or a foot cramp. Three of 'em got lost and never showed up, and the one that was aroused turned out to be a gay fan of my sister, Ruby Ann, who only wanted to see if I could get her to send him an autograph. I spent the next five days in my cabin enjoyin' the joys and wonder of my fully stocked bar.

Now, brandy is liquor distilled from wine or fermented fruit juice. Some brandies are even made from fruit pits or alcohol-soaked berries. Then it's aged in wood containers, which contributes flavor and color. The French people, bein' kind of uppity, make it from their fine wines and champagnes. The fine people of Cognac, France, make cognac brandy and there's many other countries that make brandy as well, but them French people made it famous. The name *brandy* originally meant burned wine. One thing about fruit brandies, they can age in a short time right in the bottle. Now that's my kind of liquor!

APPLE BRANDY COCKTAIL

1½ ounces apple brandy
1 teaspoon grenadine
1 teaspoon lemon juice

Shake with ice and strain into a chilled cocktail glass.

APRICOT COCKTAIL

1½ ounces apricot-flavored brandy
Splash of gin
Juice of ¼ lemon
Juice of ½ orange

Shake with ice and strain into a cocktail glass.

AWESOME CHERRY BLOSSOM

½ ounce cherry-flavored brandy
2 tablespoons powdered sugar
1½ ounces brandy
1½ teaspoons triple sec
1½ teaspoons grenadine
2 teaspoons lemon juice
Maraschino cherry for garnish

Moistened the rim of a cocktail glass with the cherry brandy and dip it into powdered sugar (page 36). Shake the ingredients with ice and strain into the glass. Put the cherry on top.

BABY DOLL

2 ounces brandy or cognac
1½ ounces Grand Marnier
Juice of ½ lemon
Powdered sugar

Stir the liquors and lemon juice over ice gently. Strain into a chilled cocktail glass with a sugar rim (page 36).

BAD HABIT

¼ ounce brandy
¼ ounce vodka
¼ ounce Grand Marnier
¼ ounce curaçao
Juice of 1 lime
3 ounces sour mix

Shake and strain into a highball glass with ice.

BEDROOM RAIDER

4 ounces brandy
2 ounces vodka
2 ounces Hot Damn
6 ounces Kahlúa
Orange juice

Mix the first four ingredients in a tall glass and top it off with orange juice.

BEE STING

1¼ ounces blackberry brandy
¾ ounce white crème de menthe

Shake with ice and strain into a chilled cocktail glass.

BETWEEN THE SHEETS

¾ ounce brandy
¾ ounce light rum
¾ ounce lemon juice
½ ounce triple sec

Shake with ice and strain into a chilled cocktail glass.

BRANDY ALEXANDER (UP)

½ ounce brandy
½ ounce brown crème de cacao
1 ounce light cream or milk

Shake with ice and strain into a chilled cocktail glass.

BRANDY COLLINS

2 ounces brandy
Juice of ½ lemon
2 teaspoons powdered sugar
Club soda
Orange wedge or maraschino cherry for garnish

Shake the first three ingredients in a glass with ice. Fill the glass with club soda and stir. Top with the orange wedge or cherry.

BRANDY MILK PUNCH

2 ounces brandy
1 teaspoon powdered sugar
1 cup milk
Grated nutmeg or ground cinnamon for garnish

Shake with ice and strain into a glass. Sprinkle the nutmeg or cinnamon on top.

COLORADO CIDER

½ ounce brandy
½ ounce apple schnapps
½ ounce cinnamon schnapps (Fire Water)
Splash of apple juice

Combine all the ingredients in small snifter. Sip slowly or take as a shot.

COW IN A TWISTER

1 ounce brandy
1 ounce tequila
1 ounce vodka
1 ounce rum
1 ounce Kahlúa
1 banana
2 ounces light cream

Blend with ice until smooth and pour into a highball glass.

DEVIL IN A GREEN DRESS

1⅓ ounces brandy
1⅓ ounces green crème de menthe

Shake with ice and strain into a cocktail glass.

DEVIL'S COCKTAIL

½ ounce brandy
½ ounce apple brandy
Juice of ¼ lemon
½ ounce triple sec

Shake with ice and strain into a chilled cocktail glass.

DIRTY MOMMA

1 ounce brandy
1 ounce Kahlúa
1 ounce vodka
2 ounces half-and-half or milk

Pour the ingredients over ice and stir.

FIREBALL

¾ ounce cherry brandy
¾ ounce cinnamon schnapps (Fire Water)

Pour into a rocks glass over ice and stir.

ITALIAN SURFER

1 ounce brandy
1 ounce amaretto
Pineapple juice
Maraschino cherry for garnish

Pour the liquor into a collins glass and fill it with pineapple juice. Garnish with the cherry.

LADIES' SIDECAR

1 ounce brandy
¼ ounce triple sec
¼ ounce lemon juice
1 ounce orange juice

Shake well with ice. Strain into a chilled cocktail glass.

MAD MONKEY

2 ounces brandy
½ ounce crème de banane
½ ounce orange juice
½ ounce lemon juice

In a shaker half filled with ice cubes, combine all the ingredients. Shake well. Strain into a chilled cocktail glass.

MAYBE LATER

½ ounce brandy
½ ounce Myer's dark rum
¾ ounce Malibu rum
¾ ounce Midori melon liqueur
¾ ounce Chambord raspberry liqueur
½ ounce Bacardi 151-proof rum
½ ounce orange juice
½ ounce pineapple juice
½ ounce cranberry juice

Shake and pour into tall glass over ice.

MIDNIGHT MADNESS

1 ounce brandy
1 ounce triple sec
1 ounce Kahlúa

Pour into a rocks glass with ice and stir.

ORANGE CRUSH

¾ ounce brandy
¾ ounce orange juice
¾ ounce triple sec

Shake with ice and strain into a glass.

STINGER

1½ ounces brandy
1½ ounces white crème de menthe

Mix the ingredients with ice in a shaker and strain into a chilled cocktail glass.

SATIN SHEET

2 ounces brandy
1 ounce peach schnapps
4 ounces orange juice
1 teaspoon grenadine

Combine in a mixin' glass, stir, and pour into a collins glass filled with ice cubes.

SCOOTER

1 ounce brandy
1 ounce amaretto
1 ounce light cream

Shake all ingredients well with cracked ice, strain into a cocktail glass, and serve.

STIRRUP PANTS

1 ounce cherry brandy
1 ounce brandy
Juice of ½ lemon
1 teaspoon sugar

Shake with ice, strain into an old-fashioned glass over ice cubes, and serve.

TEED OFF

1 ounce brandy
½ ounce peppermint schnapps
1½ ounces pineapple juice
1½ ounces orange juice

Shake with ice and strain into a chilled cocktail glass.

WRANGLER

1 ounce brandy
2 ounces sloe gin
2 ounces Malibu rum
6 ounces Coca-Cola
Splash of grenadine

Pour in a highball glass with ice and stir.

Chapter 6

Nothin' complements the show you'll see when you come to the Blue Whale
Strip Club more than the world-famous house specialty, the Fish Basket.

Foods Right Off the Menu

Back when we was tryin' to get Flora Delight to join our happy band of Blue Whale girls, we knew it'd take a lot to drag her from Birmingham, but with the talent that she's got, we just had to have her. So I talked her into comin' on up to visit us just for a few days, although at first she said thank you but no. Of course I've never been one to take a no from anybody, just ask most of the men who've ended up at my trailer after I've worked my sexy ways on 'em and then got 'em good and drunk. But Flora was gonna be a lot harder to seduce since she had a reputation all along the stripper circuit of bein' able to drink even the likes of Boris Yeltzin under the table. So that was out. But I wasn't down yet. I pulled out all the guns and called Flora back and this time I sweetened the offer with the one thing a professional exotic dancer is hard pressed to turn down, a free round-trip bus ticket. I had to bend over backward to get Melba to finally agree to pay the $98 seven-day-advanced-purchase fare, but I knew it would all be well worth it. I don't know if it's the fact that the people on the bus treat strippers like royalty since most of 'em have seen us perform before, or if it's simply on account of the first-class feel that you get from bein' driven around. In any case, I'd managed to get my foot in Flora Delight's door, so to speak.

Two weeks later, after a fourteen-hour ride, she was walkin' in the door of the Blue Whale. All us girls had decorated the place up real nice. We wanted to hang streamers from the ceilin', but none of us dared to try and climb a ladder, so instead we all jumped in and made her a big welcome sign out of pull tabs and beer bottle caps. It was real pretty and after we'd finished blowin' up the balloons, the bar looked real nice. And in her honor, we even wrote Flora's motel room number on the men's bathroom

76

wall. Needless to say, Flora was floored at our good old Arkansas hospitality and the fact that we'd pulled out all the stops for her. And of course, she was already in a good mood on account of her bus trip. She'd romanced three men and one of 'em was even awake, and disarmed a knife-wieldin' psycho before romancin' him as well. So you can imagine the good spirits that she was in.

I gave Flora a tour of the Blue Whale and introduced her to the staff. Then I took her back to the dressin' room and helped her unpack. She had some of the nicest boas that I've ever seen. Obviously we wasn't dealin' with some cheap lush who liked to take her clothes off in public. No, Flora was definitely all we'd heard about her.

Come show time, Flora was ready to do her first number, which was called Steam Heat. She had this specially made glittery sequined bra/harness as well as a special pink boa that she wore for this song. When the lyrics would say the words *steam heat* she'd push this hidden button that'd cause a big burst of steam to shoot out from each pasty on the bra. Oh it was somethin', and with the exception of those two fellas that got scalded and were rushed to the emergency on account of Flora not bein' used to workin' so close to the audience, everybody just loved it.

Her second number, "Tie a Yellow Ribbon Around the Old Oak Tree," was killer too. She came out in nothin' but a pair of yellow pasties, a yellow thong, and a big yellow boa. And she had these great big yellow ribbons all in her hair. When a fella would tip her, she'd take a ribbon from her hair and give it to him so he could tie it around her wooden leg. Did I forget to mention that she has a wooden leg? It keeps slippin' my mind that not every one of y'all is a big stripper fan. Sorry about that. But anyways, everyone loved that song as well. Actually, she slayed 'em with every number that she did, and when the night was over, she'd made almost $14 in change and $6 in actual dollar bills. That was the most money that any of us had made on a Tuesday night.

Even though the crowd had gone wild and tipped her well, Flora announced that her heart was still in Birmingham with her sickly eighty-nine-year-old mother. She'd love to move here, but, well, her mother just wouldn't be able to travel on account of her health. We was all disappointed and told her that maybe later on in the future if things should change for her she could come back and join our cast. Before we could all break down and cry, chef Bernie came back and told us that he'd made a meal for all of us in honor of Flora's goin' away. Not bein' one to question a free meal, we all quickly moved into the club area and dived in. Chef Bernie served up his Dockside Corn Sticks, Teeny-Weeny Jambalaya, and a slice of his Bump and Grind Cake. As she tore into that wonderful spread, Flora asked if chef Bernie always made food this good. Of course we all said yes and we mentioned our favorite dishes that he prepared. Well, as fate would have it, before she'd finished off her Bump and Grind Cake, Flora had announced that she'd love to take us up on our offer to become a Blue Whale girl. When I asked her if she thought the move would be safe for her mother, she replied that the old woman had enjoyed a good and happy life, and "if she dies, she dies." As y'all will soon find out from the food items, which come directly off the menu at the Blue Whale Strip Club, it's hard to say no to chef Bernie's cookin'.

Now before you dive into these recipes, let me tell y'all about our house special. It's called the Fish Basket, and y'all might recall seein' in *Ruby Ann's Down Home Trailer Park Cookbook* my sister, Ruby Ann's husband, Dew, wearin' the classy T-shirt that reads I ATE THE FISH BASKET AT THE BLUE WHALE STRIP CLUB (you can also order this same shirt by goin' to the Blue Whale's Web page at www.rubylot18.homestead.com/bluewhale.html). Basically you get six pounds of catfish, fries, and a side of slaw for only 99¢. I don't know why they sell it so cheap, but it sure does seem to keep them folks comin' in to the bar. Anyhow, enjoy!

APPETIZERS

DOCKSIDE CORNSTICKS

These are so good, I accept 'em as tips.

Serves 4 to 6

1 cup cornmeal, sifted
¼ teaspoon salt
¼ teaspoon bakin' soda
4 tablespoons cookin' oil
1 cup buttermilk
2½ tablespoons light corn syrup

Take your sifted cornmeal and mix in the salt and bakin' soda. Add the rest of the ingredients and mix well. Pour the batter into a greased corn stick pan. If you ain't got that, pour the batter into a long greased cake pan. Cook for 40 minutes at 400 degrees F. If you use a cake pan, dump it out and make your own corn sticks by cutting long strips.

UNDER THE SEA PICKLED EGGS

Any bar worth its weight has to have a good pickled egg.

Makes 2 dozen eggs

4 cups white vinegar
2 teaspoons salt
2 teaspoons crushed bay leaves
½ cup sugar

2½ tablespoons picklin' spices

2 dozen hard-boiled eggs

Combine the first five ingredients in a big pot and bring to a boil. While it's heatin' up, shell your eggs. Place the eggs in a large bowl or jar. Pour the hot vinegar mixture over the eggs, cover, and put in the fridge. Serve cold.

OCEANS OF THE WORLD ONION DIP

This dip is out of this world!

Makes about 6 cups

2 cups sugar

½ cup white vinegar

2½ cups water

6 onions, finely diced

¾ cup mayonnaise

1 teaspoon seasonin' salt

In a large bowl, put the first three ingredients. Stir well. Add the onions, and let 'em soak for 3 hours. Drain and add the mayonnaise and seasonin' salt. Mix well and serve.

SAIL AWAY SHRIMP DIP

I don't like shrimp, but all the other girls just love this stuff.

Makes 4 to 6 cups

1 pound boiled medium shrimp, peeled and deveined

1 hard-boiled egg, chopped

3 ounces cream cheese

½ cup margarine

¼ chopped onion

¼ cup mayonnaise

1 clove garlic

1 teaspoon Worcestershire sauce

¼ teaspoon salt

⅛ teaspoon pepper

Throw everything into a food processor and let it go until it makes a nice smooth mixture. Put it into a big bowl and cover. Place in the fridge for 3 to 5 hours. Scoop out servin' portions and serve.

LITTLE LINDA NACHOS

They don't get much bigger than these nachos.

Serves 4 to 6

1 regular can chili

1 regular can Cheddar cheese soup

1 cup salsa

1 big bag tortilla chips

1 tomato, chopped

1 onion, chopped

Mix together the chili, cheese soup, and salsa in a big bowl. Microwave for 2 minutes, stir, cook for 2 more minutes, stir, and cook one last time for an additional 2 minutes. Set aside.

Place a layer of chips on a big plate. Spread some of the sauce on the chips. Sprinkle on some of the tomatoes and onions. Top this with more chips and more sauce, tomatoes, and onions. Continue the layerin', makin' each one a little smaller in size than the one before. You should have a small tower of nachos when you're done.

SOUP

BOTTOM OF THE SEA CHILI

This is quick and easy, just like me.

Serves 6 to 8

2 pounds hamburger meat
1 cup chopped onion
2 large cans stewed tomatoes
1 large can kidney beans
2 tablespoons chili powder
1 regular can tomato sauce
2 tablespoons sugar
1 tablespoon vinegar
2 teaspoons garlic powder
1 teaspoon salt

Brown the meat and onions together in a skillet. Drain off your grease and add the other ingredients. Cover and let simmer for 30 minutes.

MELBA'S GRANNY BERRY'S BEER-CHEESE SOUP

Melba says that her gospel-singin' granny would boil the hell out of the beer so it would be all right for a good southern Baptist to enjoy.

Serves 4 to 6

2 cups margarine
½ cup minced celery
½ cup grated carrots
½ cup finely diced onions
½ cup flour
5 cups chicken broth
½ teaspoon dry mustard

2 cups Velveeta, cubed
1 can beer
1 teaspoon salt
½ teaspoon pepper

Put your margarine into a hot skillet and add the vegetables. Sauté the little buggers until they get slightly tender. Add your flour and stir over a low heat until it expands. Stirrin' constantly, add the chicken broth, a little at a time. When it thickens, stop stirrin' and let it simmer for 4 to 5 minutes. Add your mustard and then put in your Velveeta and stir till it melts, then follow up with your beer. Stir to blend. Add your salt and pepper and stir. Let it simmer for 3 to 6 minutes.

TEENY-WEENY JAMBALAYA

Flora can eat this stuff till she's close to explodin'.

Makes about 6 servin's

2 tablespoons margarine
1 pound cocktail sausages
½ cup chopped onions
½ cup chopped celery
½ cup chopped green bell pepper
1 (28-ounce) can whole tomatoes with the juice
3 cups cooked rice
½ teaspoon garlic powder
½ teaspoon red pepper flakes
½ teaspoon thyme

Melt the margarine in a skillet and sauté the next four ingredients, stirrin' until the sausages are brown. Drain the tomato juice into the mixture.

Take the tomatoes and chop 'em up. Add to the mixture followed by the rest of the ingredients. Stir and cook for 5 to 7 more minutes.

BURGERS

THE BLUE WHALE BURGER

Forget the dang Fish Basket, this one is my favorite.

Makes 8 burgers

2 pounds hamburger meat
2 dill pickles, chopped up real good
3 ounces stuffin' mix
1 onion, finely chopped
Dash of salt
Dash of pepper
3 tablespoons vegetable oil
8 hamburger buns
8 tablespoons sweet corn relish (recipe below)
1 cup shredded Cheddar cheese

With your hands, mix the hamburger, pickles, stuffin' mix, and onions together. Shape into 8 burgers. Salt and pepper each one. Put the oil in a skillet and fry up your burgers till they're done. Toast your buns. Put the burgers on 'em and top with corn relish and Cheddar cheese. Serve with your favorite condiments.

CHEF BERNIE'S SECRET SWEET CORN RELISH

So much for his secret!

Makes 8 to 9 cups

4 tablespoons olive oil
6 tablespoons cider vinegar
2 tablespoons honey
½ teaspoon ground cumin

½ teaspoon pepper
4 cups sweet corn
1 cup chopped red bell pepper
1 cup chopped green onion
2 large tomatoes, chopped

Mix together the first five ingredients and set aside.

Cook up your corn. Stir it into the mixture you set aside. Add the peppers, onions, and tomatoes. Stir well. Cover it and keep it in the fridge.

THE BARNACLE BURGER

Flora can eat three of these at one settin'.

Makes 4 burgers

1 pound ground beef
3 tablespoons ketchup
1 teaspoon prepared mustard
1 small onion, finely chopped
1 teaspoon salt
½ cup soft bread crumbs
¼ cup milk
1½ teaspoons Worcestershire sauce
4 hamburger buns
4 pickles

Mix all the ingredients except the buns together with your hands. Form into 4 patties and cook. Serve on the buns with a pickle each.

CHEF BERNIE'S PATTY MELT

Everybody just loves munchin' on a patty melt!

Makes 4 burgers

3 teaspoons margarine
1 cup chopped onions
8 slices rye bread
1 pound hamburger meat
¼ teaspoon salt
¼ teaspoon pepper
3 ounces Cheddar cheese, shredded
3 ounces Swiss cheese, shredded
4 pickles

Take 1 teaspoon of the margarine and melt it in a skillet. Add your onions and sauté 'em till tender. Set aside.

Use the remainin' margarine to spread on one side of each of the slices of bread. Set aside.

Mix your meat with the salt and pepper. Form into 4 patties and cook in the skillet.

In the meantime, combine both cheeses real good. When the burgers are done to your liking, sprinkle the cheeses evenly on them. Place a slice of bread on top of each cheesed patty with the margarine side up. Carefully turn the whole thing over and top the patty with the other slice of bread, again with the margarine side up. Let cook for a minute and then carefully flip over so the other bread can toast as well. Cook for another minute or until both sides of the sandwich are toasted. Serve each burger with a pickle.

SANDWICHES

THE CAPTAIN'S CHICKEN SALAD SANDWICHES

Ms. Amy says she'd go down with the ship for one of these.

Makes 4 sandwiches

2 cups chopped cooked chicken
1 hard-boiled egg, chopped
¼ cup chopped broccoli
5 tablespoons sweet pickle relish
4 tablespoons chopped onion
2 tablespoons mayonnaise
2 tablespoons parsley flakes
2 teaspoons Worcestershire sauce
1 teaspoon salt
¼ teaspoon pepper
8 slices white bread

Mix everything except the bread together. Spread the chicken salad on 4 pieces of bread and top with the remainin' slices. Cut the sandwiches in half and serve.

ON THE BEACH STROGANOFF SANDWICHES

I love stroganoff, don't you?

Makes 4 sandwiches

1 loaf French bread, sliced in half from end to end
1½ pounds ground beef
¼ cup chopped onion
1½ cups sour cream
1 tablespoon milk
1 teaspoon Worcestershire sauce

⅛ teaspoon garlic powder

2 tablespoons margarine, softened

1 green bell pepper, cut into rings

1 cup shredded cheese or Velveeta

½ cup pickle slices

Take your French bread and wrap it up in foil. Place it in an oven and let it bake for 12 minutes at 375 degrees F.

While you're waitin', brown the ground beef and the onions, drain, and add the next five ingredients. Stir well and let it get hot.

Your bread should be done by now, so take it out of the oven and spread your margarine on each piece. Next spread your hamburger meat mixture on one of the pieces of bread. Top this with the pepper rings and cheese. Place both pieces on a bakin' sheet in the oven for 2 minutes at 375 degrees F. Pull them out, put the pickle slices on the cheese, and place the naked piece of bread on top of the other one. Cut into 4 sections and serve.

SURF'S UP PHILLY CHEESE STEAK SANDWICH

This is almost as greasy as the fella I saw Edna French-kissin' the other night.

Makes 4 sandwiches

2 tablespoons margarine

1 large onion, diced

1 cup diced green bell pepper

1 pound round steak, sliced paper thin by the fellas in the meat department

4 ounces Cheez Whiz, melted

4 hoagie rolls, sliced from end to end

Put your margarine in a skillet and melt it on a medium heat. Add your onions and peppers, and cook for 2 to 3 minutes. Add your steak to this and keep cookin' for 2 minutes a side. Flip it all with a metal spatula and chop up the meat as it cooks. Keep doin' this until the meat is chopped up real good and cooked. Spray a nice helpin' of Cheez Whiz on the hoagie rolls. Scoop the meat mixture up and place it equally on each roll. Serve.

CHEF BERNIE'S BBQ PORK CROCK-POT SANDWICH

This is so tender, Edna can eat it without havin' to run it through the food processor first.

Makes 8 to 10 good-size sandwiches

1 medium onion, chopped up real fine
4 ounces diced green chiles
¼ teaspoon garlic powder
5-pound pork roast
1 teaspoon liquid smoke
1 cup Chef Bernie's BBQ Sauce (recipe follows)
¼ cup tomato-based chili sauce
⅓ cup apple juice
⅓ cup cider vinegar
1 teaspoon salt
1 teaspoon pepper
8 to 10 hamburger buns

Place your onions, chiles, and garlic powder in your Crock-Pot. Add the pork roast, liquid smoke, BBQ sauce, chili sauce, apple juice, vinegar, salt, and pepper. Cook, covered of course, on low for 10 hours. Take out your roast, shred it real good. Skim off the fat from the juices in the Crock-Pot, then put the shredded pork back in. Mix well. Let it cook on low for another hour or on high for 30 minutes. Serve on the buns.

CHEF BERNIE'S BBQ SAUCE

This is also good by itself with a splash of club soda and a lime twist.

Makes about 3 to 3 ½ cups

2 tablespoons margarine
1 onion, minced
½ teaspoon garlic salt
2 cups ketchup
1 teaspoon chili powder
⅓ cup lime juice
⅓ cup molasses
3 tablespoons mustard
1 tablespoon Worcestershire sauce
¾ cup rum

Melt your margarine in a skillet, add your onions and garlic salt, and let sauté for a few minutes. Pour into a pot and add everything else minus the rum. Stir well and cover. Let simmer for 20 minutes on a low heat. Add the rum. Stir and take off the heat. Let cool and bottle or put into a container to keep in your fridge.

DINNERS

THE FISH BASKET

This is the fish part, but if you go down to the vegetable section here you can get the Fish Basket Fries and Fish Basket Coleslaw recipes as well.

Makes 1 Fish basket's worth of fried catfish, which makes 4 to 6 regular servins'

½ lemon
6 pounds catfish fillets
1 tablespoon salt

½ teaspoon pepper

2¼ cups cornmeal

3 tablespoons vegetable oil

2 tablespoons hot sauce

2 tablespoons lemon juice

Take your lemon and rub it on both sides of the fillets. Set aside.

Mix the salt, pepper, and cornmeal together. Set aside.

Put your oil into a skillet and get it hot but not smokin'. Roll your fillets in the cornmeal mixture and place 'em in the hot oil. Let 'em cook till they get nice and brown on both sides.

Mix the hot sauce and lemon juice together, and spoon onto each fillet before servin'.

PARROT AND THE PIRATE PORK CHOPS AND STUFFIN'

I know some would say it's cannibalism, but I can eat a plate full of these.

Serves 3 to 6

4 to 6 pork chops

¼ cup melted margarine

2 tablespoons chopped onions

¼ cup chopped celery

¼ cup plus ⅓ can water

¼ teaspoon poultry seasonin'

3 cups soft bread cubes

1 regular can cream of chicken soup

Put your chops in a skillet and just brown both sides. Take those chops and put 'em in a bakin' dish. Set aside.

Put your margarine in a skillet and sauté the onions and celery. Take 'em out and set 'em aside.

Put the ¼ cup of water and poultry seasonin' in a bowl. Mix well. Add the sautéed onions and celery and bread cubes to this and mix again. Place the mixture on the chops and set aside.

Mix the ⅓ can of water and your soup together and pour over the chops. Stick the bakin' dish in the oven for an hour at 350 degrees F.

TASTY TUNA MELT CASSEROLE

It don't get any better than tuna melt.

Makes about 4 servin's

1 regular can cream of mushroom soup
1 regular can cream of chicken soup
2 cups cooked macaroni
6 to 7 ounces tuna fish
4 ounces Velveeta cheese, cubed into small pieces
3 tablespoons margarine
2 cups bread crumbs

Mix everything except the bread crumbs together in a big bowl. Place this mixture in a casserole dish and sprinkle the bread crumbs on top. Pop it in the oven to cook for 30 to 45 minutes at 350 degrees F.

SHIVER ME TIMBERS CHIPPED BEEF ON TOAST

This dish is very popular among our older crowd.

Makes about 4 servin's

4 ounces chipped beef
1 regular can condensed cream of mushroom soup
¼ teaspoon Worcestershire sauce
1 cup milk
Pinch of salt
¼ cup flour
4 slices toasted bread

Put the chipped beef, soup, Worcestershire sauce, and ½ cup of the milk in a pot, stir, and bring up to a boil.

Just as soon as you put the pot on the heat, combine the salt and flour in a bowl. Slowly add the remainin' milk and stir until you have a thick paste. Go back to the pot on the stove and start stirrin' until it gets to that boil. Quickly take it off the heat, add the paste, put it back on the heat, stir it all together, and bring it to a boil, stirrin' constantly. Take it off the heat and spoon out equal amounts on the slices of toast.

VEGETABLES

FISH BASKET COLESLAW

This is even better than the fish part as far as I'm concerned.

Makes enough to go with 6 fish baskets

1 cabbage, chopped up real fine
2 carrots, shredded
½ cup Miracle Whip
1½ tablespoons sugar
½ teaspoon salt
¼ teaspoon pepper

Mix the cabbage and the carrots together. Set aside.

Combine the Miracle Whip, sugar, salt, and pepper. Mix well. Add to the cabbage/carrot mix and toss. Cover the top with foil and put in the fridge till you're ready to serve.

THE FISH BASKET FRIES

Forget the ketchup, these are wonderful by themselves.

Makes enough to go with 3 fish baskets

4 bakin' potatoes, sliced into fries size
1 quart cold water
2 beef boullion cubes
½ cup sugar
2 cups vegetable oil
1 teaspoon salt
⅛ teaspoon pepper

Put the potato slices in the cold water. Add the beef boullion cubes and sugar, cover, and put in the fridge for 3 to 4 hours. After the time has passed, drain the potato slices out and dry 'em with a paper towel. Set aside.

Heat your oil up to 325 degrees F. Add your potato slices and fry till golden brown. Drain on a paper towel and sprinkle with the salt and pepper.

THAR SHE BLOWS SWEET POTATO SALAD

You don't know good till you've had some of this on your taste buds.

Serves 4 to 6

1 regular can sweet potatoes, drained
3 tablespoons Miracle Whip
½ teaspoon salt
⅛ teaspoon pepper
6 green onions, diced
1 cup diced celery
3 hard-boiled eggs, chopped

Put your sweet potatoes in a big bowl and microwave for three minutes. Stir and microwave for 1 more minute or until hot. Add your Miracle Whip and mash the potatoes. Add your salt, pepper, onions, celery, and eggs. Mix well. Cover and put in the fridge for 2 hours.

MAN OVERBOARD ONION RINGS

Ms. Amy just loves these, but she has to be careful that Slimy don't see 'em on account of how their resemblance to a hoop frightens the little bugger into a frenzy.

Makes 4 to 6 servin's

1 cup beer
2 cups flour
3 tablespoons sugar
2 teaspoons salt
1½ teaspoons seasonin' salt
4 cups shortenin'
3 onions, sliced into rings

Mix your beer and 1 cup of the flour together, then cover and let set for 3 to 4 hours out on the shelf. In the meantime, mix your sugar and salts together. After the time has passed, add your sugar mixture to the beer and flour, gently mixin' everythin' together.

Put your shortenin' in a pan and get it to 375 degrees F. Dip the onion rings into the other cup of flour and then into the batter. Carefully drop 'em a few at a time into the hot shortenin'. Cook until golden on each side. Drain on a paper towel.

DESSERTS

MELBA'S FAMOUS FROG EYE SALAD

When Melba's around, we always eat lots of this stuff.

Serves 6 to 8

1 pound acini de pepi pasta
2 tablespoons flour
1 cup sugar
2 eggs, slightly beaten
1¾ cups pineapple juice
1 tablespoon lemon juice
3 regular cans mandarin oranges
2 regular cans chunk pineapple
1 regular can crushed pineapple
1 cup miniature marshmallows
1 regular container Cool Whip
1 cup shredded coconut

Cook and drain the pasta. Set aside.

In another pan, combine the flour and sugar. Add the beaten eggs. Gradually stir in the pineapple juice. Cook over medium heat, stirrin' constantly until thickened. Add the lemon juice and let cool. Pour the sauce over the pasta and mix lightly. Refrigerate overnight. The next day, add the rest of the ingredients. Serve chilled.

BUMP AND GRIND CAKE

This is better than watchin' Little Linda try to get up on a table for a table dance.

Makes 1 cake

1 yellow cake mix
½ cup margarine, softened

3 large eggs
8 ounces cream cheese, softened
1 teaspoon vanilla extract

Combine the cake mix, margarine, and 1 egg. Pour this mixture into a 9x11-inch greased cake pan. Press it down into the pan.

Combine the rest of the ingredients in a bowl. Spread this over the pressed-down mixture. Pop it into the oven to cook for 40 minutes at 350 degrees F. No need for frostin'.

BLUE WHALE CHEESECAKE

I'll drink to this!

Makes 1 cheesecake

⅓ cup margarine, melted
1 cup graham cracker crumbs
¾ cup honey roasted peanuts, chopped up real good and fine
12 ounces cream cheese
½ cup creamy peanut butter
1 (14-ounce) can sweetened condensed milk
⅓ cup lemon juice
1 teaspoon vanilla extract
1 regular container Cool Whip

Combine the margarine, graham cracker crumbs, and peanuts. Press into the bottom of a springform pan. Stick in the fridge.

Beat your cream cheese and peanut butter until light and fluffy. Add the milk and beat until nice and smooth, then add the lemon juice and vanilla. Fold in the Cool Whip. Take the springform pan out of the fridge and put the cheese mixture into the pan. Put back in the fridge for 3 to 4 hours. When you're ready to serve, take it out of the pan.

Chapter 7

When male dancer and town mortician Vance Pool promised to take me "to heaven" durin' our date, I had no idea he meant it literally.

Gin

When I smell gin, usually on my own breath, it brings back such a swirlin' flash of memories. Now mind you, I don't necessarily mean good ones either. But as usual, they're tied to a man.

I met all four hundred pounds of Vance Poole when he came to talk to Melba Toast one evenin' about doin' a "ladies' night" on Mondays durin' football season with him and his newly formed all male review. He called his group "Vance Poole, the American Tenderloin, and His Beef Stick Boys." Accordin' to Vance, him and the boys had exotic moves that other male dancers only wished they'd thought of. Of course if Poole and his boys were a big hit, then who knows what might happen to me and the rest of the Blue Whales on Monday nights after they put the old pigskin away till next season (the football, not Vance Poole). But to be honest, me and the rest us girls were tired and really welcomed some time off since it'd been a long hot humid summer, and I was up to my eyebrows in layers of Gold Bond Medicated Powder. Anyhow, after their talk, and unbeknownst to me, Melba invited Vance to pull up a chair or two and enjoy the show that night free of charge. It wasn't until I was halfway through with my tribute to Madonna number that I our eyes met. I knew I was really workin' it like the beast that I am by just the way he gazed at me and how he tipped me $2. That should've been my warnin' sign that this man was all money and no heart. And the fact that the $2 was all in nickels and dimes should have been an omen for me as well, but oh no, that night that little dark-headed kid with the 666 on his head could have walked in and I wouldn't have caught on.

When my number was over, I grabbed my duster and threw it on. On my way to the bar to cool down, catch my breath, and get a drink, I popped

100

in a half stick of Juicy Fruit and applied another quick layer of deodorant, which I carry in my purse with me at all times. Except for his bottom and large breasts, I really didn't think he was much of a looker, but he wanted to send me a drink, and who am I to refuse a free drink? I took a long hard look at him and chugged that drink all the way down. After gaspin' for breath, I asked the bartender what the heck he'd sent me. He said it was Mr. Poole's favorite drink, a Gin Ricky with a Tricky. Well after stickin' my false eyelashes back on, I decided to go over there and thank him.

The closer I got the bigger he got! From the stage he looked like a big healthy man but I had no idea until gettin' up about three feet away that he was four hundred pounds of beef. By now I was tryin' to remember if he called his act Vance Poole and the Beef Stick Boys or the SIDE of Beef Boys! But he had a way about him that kind of turned me on. Sure I was drunk, but hey, when ain't I? Plus he flipped my switch, if you know what I mean. It was kind of like goin' to the zoo and lookin' at a rhino from behind. Sure it's got a great big bottom, but somewhere on that huge beast is a horn.

Just as I found my way to the barstool beside him, he shouted at our bartender Billy Merle to set 'em up again. He asked me to pull up a seat and we began to talk the usual small talk that men say to ladies in strip clubs; what's my sign, how long have I been a dancer, and did I have a thinner sister.

As our conversation grew, I realized we had a lot in common, both of us bein' exotic dancers and all. We kept talkin' and drinkin' for what seemed like hours. I looked up at the clock and it had been twenty minutes, but we'd done finished two more of them Gin Ricky with a Tricky things. As he signaled over to the bartender for another round for me and him, I told Billy Merle to wait, and let Vance know that in all honesty I wasn't really fond of gin. He told me that you get fewer hangovers by drinkin' gin. We'll, bein' an expert on the subject of adult beverages like I am, I wanted to know just what made him think that gin didn't give you a hangover. He told me he'd learned about gin and the lack of hangovers thereof by those who consume it while he was in medical school. I quickly ordered a double with a beer chaser. I didn't realize he was of the medical profession as well. All I could do was think about the money I'd be savin' when it comes to the cost of havin' those warts removed if I was datin' a doctor. But that dream would soon shatter as he went on to inform me about how he'd been to embalmin' school and was also a mortician. I also found out that when he works durin' the day as a mortician he uses the real spellin' of his name, Pool, so those nosy busybodies in town won't know about his secret profession.

Well, you know it makes perfect sense to me that anyone who knows how to embalm somebody must also know how to keep away a hangover. And speakin' of embalmin', after that fourth Gin Ricky double, I was the tricky, rubbin' on his neck and rather large floppy chest. But that didn't last long. Sure he loved it, but those big man breasts began to frighten me—remindin' me too much of given Me-Ma a bath.

Even as I recoiled my hands, Vance was really turnin' on the charm and ordered another round before askin' me to get up and go to the Sweet Potato Festival and Carnival with him over in Searcy. The next thing I knew we were in his '76 Plymouth Valiant and headed to the carnival. It was a nice car even though he had to hold up the driver's seat from behind with a metal baseball bat and it smelled like old cheese.

As Vance and I were enterin' the fair we were a-gigglin' like two teenagers in love. We headed over to the tunnel of love, which meant two things, he was wantin' to make out, and I'd need to take the safety off my gun. I've been robbed in that dang dark ride from hell fifteen times from men who've picked me up at the Blue Whale on various other occasions, and I was not gonna have to go down and pose for another driver's license photo for the sixteenth time in one year. Even though I didn't think it would happen with Vance, I still wasn't ready to take that chance. And as luck would have it, I never had to use my gun since the boat was so weighed down, it wouldn't even move away from the loadin' dock. We got out and Vance noticed that they had a Tilt-A-Whirl ride and suggested we give it a spin. While he went to get the tickets I stepped into the Porta Potti to freshen up.

I took a shot of Binaca and a belt of gin from one of the three flasks I'd filled up before headin' out the door at the Blue Whale, and then applied a generous coat of lipstick and deodorant just in case he was to kiss me on the ride. We boarded the Tilt-A-Whirl, grabbin' car number 9 (my lucky number out of a fortune cookie), although once he'd gotten settled in we could have used number 9½. Well, anyhow, things were startin' out great and we were smilin' at each other and laughin' as the ride started off. Soon after Vance noticed a nickel on the floor of our car. Well, the ride was gearin' up and goin' pretty fast by now even though our car wasn't a twirlin' much. It was about that time that for some reason Vance told me to hang on while he attempted to bend over to pick up that nickel. Well, between his four hundred pounds and my full-figured voluptuous body we had quite a shift of weight and that dang Tilt-A-Whirl car started spinnin' at high revolutions. Before long, I felt like a daiquiri in a blender, and pretty soon I was pinned to the back of that car like an altar boy at a clergy retreat. I was doin' my best not to panic. But then I heard a shrill, blood-curdlin' scream that grew louder and louder with each completed revolution. I thought this was odd since we was the only two on the ride. Where was that screamin' comin' from? I looked over at Vance and realized it was comin' from him! He was cryin' like a baby and screamin' like a woman in a Hitchcock film. Of course, part of the reason was on account of them there g-forces bein' so strong that it was pushin' his layers of fat up. Vance did manage to calm down for just a moment when he located the remote control to his DVD player, which he'd been searchin' for almost two weeks. But with the ever increasin' spin of that doggone out-of-control Tilt-A-Whirl car, we knew the end was near. It got so bad that poor Vance even accidentally swallowed his gold tooth!

Well, not bein' one to just lie down and take it, you know what I mean, I figured if I didn't take this matter into my own hands, then surely we'd die. So I diligently tried to push my hand down into my purse, fightin' that g-force with every inch, and pulled out my remainin' flask of gin (the first one had shot out my bra while the second one had come flyin' out of my thigh garter much earlier durin' the ride of the damned). I unscrewed the lid with my teeth and spit it out, which would prove to be a mistake since it took off flyin' at top speed and knocked out a whole row of lightbulbs, clean through the head portion of the prize winnin' margarine sculpture of President Abraham Lincoln, and finally ringin' a bell and winnin' me a giant stuffed Spuds McKenzie dog. But bein' a winner was not to last much longer—for just as I managed to beat gravity and get my flask to my lips, I heard a terrible sound that can only be described as metal meetin' metal. Somethin' had come loose and our car was rockin' and swayin' like Little Linda on tequila. As we twirled by the operator's stand I saw the carny pullin' on the big break handle with his entire body, and three people in line were helpin' him. When I heard a crashin' sound and felt several jolts to our car I realized that the bolts were coming loose and snappin' like fresh potato chips inside my pull-out love seat. I heard someone yell from out in the crowd, "Look out! It's comin' apart!" Well, I thought this was the most fun I'd ever had on a Tilt-A-Whirl in my life. We had better g-forces goin' than a space shuttle! Sparks were shootin' out from underneath all the cars and we took off like a twister in May.

The next thing I knew our car was airborne, which, when you take in to consideration the amount of weight it had in it, was a feat in itself. Well, I saw an opportunity to get some aerial advertisement, so while I was wavin' to my fans I threw out some of my business cards from the Blue Whale and from my pawnshop, The Real Easy Pawn. Within just seconds, we landed on the sidewalk and continued rollin' and bouncin' at top speeds toward the stock car track. It was nice to get a chance to unexpectedly see some of the Monster Truck Rally. But just as we got to the entrance of the track we ricocheted off a corn dog stand and headed east toward the highway. I noticed that Vance had calmed down enough to grab a couple of foot-long corn dogs and was eatin' like it was his last meal, which brings up a pet peeve of mine. Folks, I don't care what the situation is, there is never a reason to chew with your mouth open. Period!

When we hit the highway we were gainin' speed and still a spinnin' like a top. Then I heard the all-too-familiar sounds of police sirens in back of us. I could see the blue lights flashin' like a special at Kmart on a Saturday afternoon. I had to think fast. So I finished off the gin, checked my purse to make sure I had my I.D., and grabbed that other half a stick of Juicy Fruit gum to hide the smell.

The state troopers were formin' a barricade to stop us—and who knew what those boys might do when they realized I was Donna Sue Boxcar. One of the troopers threw out those spikes things to flatten our tires just like we was a stolen car or somethin'—but I guess they didn't realize that the wheels on a Tilt-A-Whirl car are made of steel. Thankfully they blew out the tires on the eighteen-wheeler in front of us, makin' the driver lose control, and his truck landed on its side with the tires facin' toward us. As luck would have it, when we hit those tires, they slowed us down, and thank goodness for that—'cause we stopped just inches away from fallin' into the duck pond. I really would have been mad, since I'd just paid $6 that day to get my hair fixed at the Beauty Barge.

Needless to say, when the troopers saw me and Vance crammed in that car they wrote us a ticket for havin' an oversized load, not wearin' seat belts, and for neglectin' to have a red flag hangin' from the back of the car and Vance's pants. We all had a good laugh, and I gave them coupons for a free Fish Basket dinner (drinks not included) at the Whale for givin' us a ride back to the carnival. I think one of them was even makin' eyes at me in the rearview mirror.

Vance and I went back to the Blue Whale after our adventure to tell everyone what a grand time we'd had. Of course in the long run we didn't work out. Vance, you see, has a drinkin' problem. He don't like to share his cocktails even with the person he loves when they've finished their beverage and are waitin' for the bartender to make 'em a new one. Plus he turned out to be too hot for me to handle. Not only is he the town mortician, but now he and the Beef Stick Boys work here at the Blue Whale on Monday nights durin' football season. It gives us the night off and the women in the surroundin' area somethin' to throw themselves at. Of course the 5¢ margaritas don't drive the gals away either.

I put my big Spuds McKenzie dog up on the shelf behind the bar, and every time I see it durin' a long hard day of bein' sexy, I order up a Gin Ricky with a Tricky just for old times' sake, and I toast what might have been, if only the man I loved wasn't loved by all on Monday nights.

In Arkansas durin' the winter we don't get much snow; we get ice storms. Well, one time when we were all iced in and I couldn't get to the club I stumbled, slipped, and slid over to Ruby Ann's trailer to check out her liquor cabinet. Since she had a few pieces of bottles left over from New Year's and she's got cable, I decided to stay for a while and started watchin' one of them educational shows. What caught my attention was they were talkin' about the history of gin.

Now, I was really sittin' up and takin' notice when they said that originally gin was invented for medical reasons as a treatment for kidney disorders. After pourin' another tall one I watched as they told about the soldiers takin' a likin' to it, and the thought of a gin-soaked military man was warmin' me up on a cold winter's night. They went on to say the original gins used to be sweetened and I was beginnin' to long for the good ol' days. I must have missed somethin' while I was makin' another drink 'cause they'd moved on to Prohibition, when people were forced to make their own gin in their bathtubs. That sure beats washin' out knee highs any day. About the time they were gonna tell the recipe the ice storm knocked out the power, but I know that gin is made from grain and distilled like vodka and favored with juniper—and I'd kill for that recipe.

BACHELOR BAIT

2 ounces gin
1 ounce orange juice
1 ounce pineapple juice
Dash of grenadine

Shake with cracked ice and strain into a chilled cocktail glass.

BEAUTY BARGE SPECIAL

1½ ounces gin
1 ounce apricot-flavored brandy
1½ teaspoons grenadine

½ ounce triple sec
Juice of ½ orange
Juice of ½ lemon
1 teaspoon powdered sugar

Shake with ice, strain into a glass half filled with ice cubes, and serve.

BING, BANG, BOOM!

1 shot gin
1 shot vodka
1 shot peach schnapps
1 shot cinnamon schnapps
1 shot rum

Mix in shaker with ice and strain into a rocks glass.

BLUE MOON OF KENTUCKY

1½ ounces gin
¾ ounces blue curaçao
Lemon twist for garnish

Stir with ice and strain into a cocktail glass. Add the lemon twist.

BLUE WHALE MARTINI

3 ounces gin
½ ounce blue curaçao
Lemon twist for garnish

Stir well over ice cubes and strain into a chilled cocktail glass. Add the lemon twist.

COME TO MOMMA!

1 ounce gin
1 ounce vodka
1 ounce sour mix
1 ounce grenadine
Beer

Mix the gin, vodka, sour mix, and grenadine together in shaker and pour into a tall glass with ice. Top off the glass with beer.

DEFERRED SENTENCE

1 ounce gin
1 ounce cherry vodka
1 ounce Jack Daniel's
½ ounce 151-proof rum

Pour into a shaker with ice. Strain into a chilled martini glass.

DEW BE CAREFUL

1 ounce gin
½ ounce Cointreau
½ ounce grenadine
Splash of Mountain Dew

Shake with ice and strain into a cocktail glass.

DONNA SUE'S BIRTHSTONE COCKTAIL (AMETHYST COCKTAIL)

1 ounce gin
½ ounce Chambord raspberry liqueur
2 ounces pineapple juice

Shake with ice and strain into a chilled martini glass.

DRY MARTINI

2 ounces gin
Dash of dry vermouth
Olives for garnish

Add the gin and vermouth to a mixin' glass with ice. Strain into a chilled cocktail or martini glass. Add a couple of olives on a toothpick for garnish.

GIBSON

2½ ounces gin
¼ ounce dry vermouth
Cocktail onions on a stick for garnish

Stir with cubed ice and strain over the onions into a chilled martini glass.

GIMLET

1 ounce gin
2 ounces lime juice
1 teaspoon sugar
Lime juice for garnish

Mix and serve in a rocks glass over ice. Garnish with a squeeze of lime juice.

GIN RICKEY

1½ ounces gin
Club soda
Juice of ½ lime

Pour the gin into a chilled highball glass over ice cubes. Fill it with club soda. Add the lime juice and stir.

GIN RICKEY WITH A TRICKEY

2 ounces gin
2 ounces sloe gin
Juice of ¼ lime
Splash of Rose's Lime Juice
Splash of soda water

Pour all the ingredients into a shaker with ice. Shake and strain into a chilled martini glass.

GUTTER TRASH

1½ ounces gin
1 tablespoon orange juice
Splash of brandy
Splash of grenadine

Shake with ice and strain into a rocks glass.

KISS IN THE NIGHT

½ ounce gin
½ ounce cherry-flavored brandy
½ ounce peach schnapps
Splash of orange juice

Shake with ice and strain into a chilled martini glass.

MANHANDLED

1½ ounces gin
3 ounces Homemade Sweet 'n' Sour Mix (page 147)
1 teaspoon sugar

½ ounce grenadine
1 ounce club soda

Shake the gin, sweet 'n' sour mix, and sugar. Pour into a collins glass over ice. Add the grenadine and fill with the club soda. Stir!

MAY I ADDRESS THE COURT?

1 ounce gin
1 ounce Bacardi 151-proof rum
1 ounce tequila
1 ounce bourbon
1 ounce vodka
1 ounce Irish whiskey
1 ounce Midori melon liqueur
Coca-Cola

Combine the first seven ingredients in a highball glass over ice. Top it off with Coca-Cola.

MINT MARTINI

2 ounces gin
1 ounce white crème de menthe

In a mixin' jar half filled with ice cubes, combine the gin and crème de menthe. Stir well and strain into a chilled cocktail glass.

OPAL'S ORANGE JUICE

1½ ounces gin
½ ounce triple sec
1 ounce orange juice
¼ tablespoon powdered sugar

Shake with ice and strain into a chilled martini glass.

ORANGE BLOSSOM SPECIAL

1½ ounces gin
½ ounce cherry brandy
4 ounces orange juice
Ginger ale

Shake the gin, brandy, and orange juice and pour into a highball glass over ice cubes. Fill it with ginger ale and stir gently.

PANGBURN PINK LEMONADE

1 ounce gin
1 ounce vodka
3 ounces pink lemonade
Can of beer

Pour the gin, vodka, and lemonade into a tall glass with ice. Fill it with the beer.

PASTIE TWISTER

1 ounce gin
1 ounce tequila
1 ounce Rose's Lime Juice
Maraschino cherry for garnish

Pour into a rocks glass over crushed ice and garnish with the cherry.

RASPBERRY LONG ISLAND ICED TEA

1 ounce gin
1 ounce vodka
1 ounce rum
1 ounce triple sec

1½ ounces Homemade Sweet 'n' Sour Mix (page 147)
1 ounce Chambord raspberry liqueur
Lemon juice for garnish

Pour all the ingredients into a shaker over ice. Pour into a tall glass and garnish with the squeeze of a lemon.

RED RACE CAR

½ ounce gin
½ ounce vodka
½ ounce rum
½ ounce Grand Marnier
Surge soda
Grenadine

Pour the first four ingredients into a tall glass over ice. Fill it with the soda and top it off with grenadine. Stir well.

RED SNAPPER

2 ounces gin
4 ounces tomato juice
½ ounce lemon juice
2 to 3 dashes of Worcestershire sauce
2 to 3 drops of Tabasco sauce
Pinch of salt and pepper

Stir the ingredients with cracked ice in a chilled hurricane glass.

RUBY'S ROCKIN' ROOT BEER

2 ounces gin
1 ounce lemon juice
1 teaspoon superfine sugar

4 ounces root beer

Maraschino cherry for garnish

In a shaker, combine the gin, lemon juice, and sugar. Shake well. Strain into a collins glass almost filled with ice cubes. Add the root beer. Stir well. Garnish with the cherry.

SALTY DOG

1 ounce gin

4 ounces grapefruit juice

Serve on the rocks in a glass with a salted rim (page 36).

SINGAPORE SLING

2 ounces gin

1 ounce cherry brandy

Juice of ½ lemon

½ teaspoon powdered sugar

Club soda

Mix the gin, brandy, lemon juice, and sugar in a shaker. Pour into a collins glass over ice. Fill it with club soda.

STRIPPER'S SLIPPER

1 ounce gin

½ ounce triple sec

2 ounces cranberry juice

1 ounce grapefruit juice

1 ounce Sprite

Lemon slice for garnish

Maraschino cherry for garnish

Shake with ice and strain into a cocktail glass. Garnish with the lemon slice and cherry.

SUMMER SUNSET

2 shots gin
1 shot triple sec
Pineapple juice
Splash of grenadine

Fill a glass with crushed ice. Add the gin and triple sec and fill it with pineapple juice. Add the splash of grenadine on top.

THUNDER THONG

1 ounce gin
1 ounce brandy
1 ounce whiskey
1 ounce dry vermouth
Splash of orange juice

Shake and strain into a highball glass with ice.

TIP MONEY

1½ ounces gin
1 ounce green crème de menthe
Squeeze of lime juice

Shake all the ingredients and strain into a rocks glass over ice.

TOM COLLINS

2 ounces gin
3 ounces Homemade Sweet 'n' Sour Mix (page 147)
Splash of 7UP
Maraschino cherry for garnish

Shake and strain into a collins glass filled with ice. Add the cherry on top.

TRUTH SERUM

2 ounces gin
2 ounces rum
2 ounces vodka
2 ounces pineapple juice
2 ounces grapefruit juice
1½ ounces grenadine

Mix in shaker and pour over ice into a tall glass.

WHITE SPIDER

1 ounce gin
1 ounce sour mix
½ ounce triple sec

Shake the ingredients with ice, then strain into a cocktail glass.

Chapter 8

I'm goin' to Kansas City—Kansas City, here I come!

After-Dinner Drinks, Hot Drinks, and Frozen Drinks

Every year in December everybody at The High Chaparral Trailer Park, where I reside over in Lot #6, all gather together and hold our traditional evenin' Christmas carolin'. Now since we only got twenty lots total, it really don't take us any more than about an hour tops to make the round. And I typically just go in late that night to work after we've finished. Since the good Lord seen fit to bless me and my sister, Ruby Ann, with oral talents, watch it, I always have enjoyed this night. Usually what'll happen is that one of the lots in the trailer park will make up a big batch of hot chocolate for us all to put in our thermoses to enjoy and carry with us as we sing from empty trailer to empty trailer since everyone who lives there is raisin' their voices in song. The heat from both the hot chocolate as well as the massive Christmas lights on each trailer home helps to keep us warm and in good spirits. Of course last year our spirits were the highest they'd ever been, thanks to Donny Owens and Kenny Lynn of Lot #15.

Donny and Kenny are real sweet guys who love life, canasta, sewin', and antiques. They're also real fun to party with and have a great sense of humor, but for some reason they won't go no further than friends with me. Trust me, I've used all my feminine and unfeminine ways to try and scoop these boys up, but no go. All of us at the High Chaparral think that their religion makes 'em shun relations with the opposite sex, sort of like a vow of chastity. We ain't sure if that's the case or not seein' how there ain't all that many Episcopalians in the Pangburn area besides them. Anyways, they volunteered to do the hot chocolate this past Christmas, which was really good. They used some top-of-the-line mix and had even made some of their homemade Irish Crème to add to the hot drink to give it an even better taste. Of course both Kenny and Donny as well as myself just as-

118

sumed everyone knew Irish Crème had alcohol in it, which was why they asked everybody if they wanted the Irish Crème added to their thermoses or if they just wanted it plain. Of course they all wanted the Irish Crème, and with it tastin' so yummy, it's easy to understand why. Well, for some reason or another, it was an extremely cold and bitter evenin' so by the third trailer we'd all drunk up our hot chocolate. Kenny and Donny said for us not to worry, so we made a brief pit stop back at Lot #15. While the boys whipped up another quick batch, we all did a few Christmas carols for 'em. Then we refilled our thermoses and got back to our carolin' of the empty trailer homes. Well, by Lot #8 the effects of the liquor was finally startin' to kick in. Some folks were swayin' while others were findin' it hard to focus on the printed song lyrics. As for me, well, I was already down. These Irish Crème hot chocolates had put me away to the point of where I couldn't stand. Of course the bottle of vodka I'd brought along probably had a little bit to do with it as well, but don't quote me on that. Anyways, not wantin' to be a party pooper, I had my niece tie me down to the kiddie sled, which she don't use no more, and with carols in hand, I sang along as her and her boyfriend, Billy Bob, pulled me and my beverages along with the group.

"To hell with Lot number ten, " Sister Bertha slurred as we started into "Deck the Halls" in front of dear old Ollie White's mobile home, "she's just a dang widow woman. Let's go back to fifteen for some more hot chocolate. I need a refill!" For the first time in my life, I couldn't have agreed with Sister Bertha more. Even Ollie White raised her voice in agreement, and led the march of the drunken fools back to Lot #15. Donny and Kenny whipped up another batch while Sister Bertha went off on some kind of rampage, sharin' all the gossip that she knows about everybody in town. If she could have stood up, I know Pastor Ida May Bee would've told her to shut up since she don't like all that talkin' about people. She a good woman and a wonderful pastor who always comes by my trailer to make sure I'm doin' all right. Because of her, I've actually been goin' back to church from time to time. Anyhow, in what seemed like only seconds later the boys were back outside with the scaldin' hot chocolate and Irish Crème. Then we were off.

Skippin' Lots 11 through 14 by a unanimous decision, we left Lot #15 and started on Lot #16. When we finally made it to my sister's pink two-story double-wide in Lot #18 we were no longer able to actually sing the words, at least not in English, and unbeknownst to most of us, we were mumblin' three different songs at one time. I think three and a half hours later Kenny, Donny, Dick Inman of Lot #1, and Ben Beaver of Lot #14, who owns Beaver Liquors and Wines and manages the trailer park, were the only people who actually made it to Lot #20. Even the Birches, who lived there at the time, had made a bed for the night on the sofa and love seat at one of the other trailers. As a matter of fact, most folks didn't make it back to their trailers that night. Mind you, there was no hanky-panky goin' on, they just couldn't walk no farther without runnin' into somethin'. As for me, well, I don't know exactly what happened, but I woke up the next day on that sled, which was attached to the bumper of a Ford Expedition parked in a truck stop just outside Kansas City. But don't worry, 'cause two days later after I'd snuck into the back of a Mayflower movin' van, I was back home in time for Christmas. We would've been back earlier, but I fell asleep on a Sealy Posturepedic bed that was in the back of that dang van and didn't wake up until Joplin, where I was able to find a club to do a guest spot at and make enough money to catch a bus back to Pangburn. Of course the kiddie sled didn't make it back on account of me pawnin' it. Between that and me sellin' a pint of blood I was able to get a meal and a bottle. Sister Bertha led the petition to change the way our trailer park carolin' is done so that Kenny and Donny could do their "special hot chocolate" every year. Needless to say, the change was easily voted in at our January trailer park community meetin'.

Now you may like your cordials and after-dinner drinks frozen, straight up, or in coffee. You also may want to try makin' some of your own liqueurs. So I have divided this chapter into several sections, startin' with after-dinner drinks. Some of these can be served straight up and some with cream or in coffee—or for a tasty dessert try mixin' some with ice cream.

Liqueurs are made by flavorin' liquor with various parts of plants, flowers, fruit, and leaves. You can't just use anything, though, so be careful. I tried dandelions one time, and had to use a "weed be gone" spray on my legs for nearly six months. Liqueurs also have sugar, and lots of it. The most popular flavors to make liqueur from are oranges (triple sec, Cointreau), apricots, coffee, blackberries, cherries, chocolate (crème de cacao, Baileys), peaches, and peppermint. Don't be afraid to try some of these store-bought ones if you've got a lot of money. I also included some homemade recipes at the end of this chapter. Just remember to watch how much you drink of these things. Not only will they sneak up on you, but to be honest I once drank so much of that liqueur that's got them gold flakes in it that the next day I passed a bracelet and a pair of hoop earrings. There is a list in chapter 2 under the "Stockin' Your Bar" section which tells you what these taste like or what they're made from.

AFTER DINNER DRINKS

BANANA BANSHEE

1 ounce banana liqueur
1 ounce white crème de cacao
2 ounces light cream

Shake with ice and strain into a chilled cocktail glass.

BANANA CREAM PIE

1 ounce Malibu coconut rum
1 ounce banana liqueur
4 ounces pineapple juice

The ingredients can be served on the rocks in a highball glass or put into a blender with ice and served frozen.

BANANA SPLIT

1 ounce banana liqueur
1 ounce Irish cream
½ ounce chocolate liqueur
2 ounces light cream

Shake with ice and strain into a chilled cocktail glass.

BLUE ANGEL

1 ounce brandy
½ ounce blue curaçao
½ ounce vanilla liqueur
½ ounce half-and-half

Shake with ice and strain into a chilled cocktail glass.

BRANDY ALEXANDER (ICE CREAM)

½ ounce brandy
½ ounce light crème de cacao
2 ounces light cream
Dash of grated nutmeg for garnish

Shake with ice and strain into a chilled cocktail glass. Top with the nutmeg.

DONNA SUE'S ROOT BEER FLOAT

Scoop of vanilla ice cream
1 ounce vodka
1 ounce root beer schnapps
Root beer

Put the ice cream in a tall wide-mouthed glass, add the vodka and root beer schnapps, then fill with root beer.

FROZEN FRUITY

1 ounce Midori melon liqueur
1 ounce curaçao
1 ounce Frangelico
½ ounce strawberry liqueur
½ ounce Tia Maria
2 ounces light cream
grenadine for garnish

Blend with ice until smooth, pour into a brandy snifter, and top with a drizzle of grenadine.

GOLDEN CADILLAC

½ ounce Galliano
½ ounce light crème de cacao
2 ounces light cream

Shake with ice and strain into a chilled cocktail glass.

GRASSHOPPER

½ ounce green crème de menthe
½ ounce light crème de cacao
2 ounces light cream

Shake with ice and strain into a chilled cocktail glass.

MACAROON

2 ounces vodka
½ ounce Malibu rum
½ ounce chocolate liqueur
½ ounce amaretto

Stir with cracked ice and strain into a chilled cocktail glass.

PINK SQUIRREL

½ ounce crème de noyaux
½ ounce light crème de cacao
2 ounces light cream

Shake with ice and strain into a chilled cocktail glass.

VANILLA DR PEPPER ON THE WILD SIDE

2 ounces Frangelico
12 ounces Dr Pepper

Mix in a highball glass with ice.

VELVET HAMMER

1 ounce vodka
1 ounce crème de cacao
2 ounces light cream

Shake with ice and strain into a chilled cocktail glass.

HOT DRINKS

BARN BURNER

1½ ounces Southern Comfort
Cinnamon stick
Lemon twist
1 cup hot cider

Put the Southern Comfort, cinnamon stick, and lemon twist in a mug and add the hot cider.

BUN WARMER

¾ ounce apricot brandy
¾ ounce Southern Comfort
Cinnamon stick
Hot apple cider

Put the brandy, Southern Comfort, and cinnamon stick in a coffee mug. Fill the mug with hot cider.

CHOCOLATE COFFEE KISS

¾ ounce coffee liqueur
¾ ounce Irish cream
Splash of brown crème de cacao
Splash of Grand Marnier
1½ ounces chocolate syrup
Hot coffee
Whipped cream for garnish
Shaved chocolate for garnish
Maraschino cherry for garnish

Pour the liqueurs and chocolate syrup into a coffee mug and fill it up with coffee. Top with the whipped cream, shaved chocolate, and cherry.

CINNAMON TOAST

1¼ ounces Captain Morgan spiced rum
1 ounce Irish cream
1 ounce Goldschlager
6 ounces hot apple cider

Pour the rum, Irish cream, and Goldschlager into a tall coffee mug. Add the hot apple cider and stir.

COMMON COLD MEDICINE

6 ounces warm milk
1½ ounces scotch
1 teaspoon butter

Put the warm milk in a mug and add the scotch and butter. Mix and sip. (This will warm you all over and make you sleep like a baby.)

HOT BUTTERED RUM

1 teaspoon brown sugar
Boilin' water
1 tablespoon butter
2 ounces dark rum
Nutmeg for garnish

Pour the sugar into a cup and fill two-thirds full with boilin' water. Add the butter and rum. Stir and sprinkle the nutmeg over the top.

HOT BUTTERED RUM MIX

16 to 18 servin's

1 cup sugar
1 cup brown sugar, packed
1 cup butter
2 cups vanilla ice cream
1 cup rum
Boilin' water
Nutmeg for garnish

In 2-quart saucepan, combine the sugar, brown sugar, and butter. Cook over low heat, stirrin' occasionally, until butter is melted, 6 to 8 minutes. In large mixin' bowl, combine the cooked mixture with the ice cream, beat at medium speed, scrapin' the bowl often until smooth, 1 to 2 minutes. Store refrigerated up to 2 weeks or frozen up to 1 month. For each servin', fill a mug with ¼ cup of the ice cream mixture, 1 ounce rum, and ¾ cup boilin' water, then sprinkle with nutmeg.

HOT FRENCH KISS

½ ounce triple sec
½ ounce amaretto
¼ ounce Irish cream
5 ounces coffee
Whipped cream for garnish

Pour the liqueurs into a tall mug and fill it up with strong coffee. Top with whipped cream.

HOT SCHNAPPOLATE

1½ ounces peppermint schnapps
1 cup hot cocoa
1 tablespoon whipped cream

Pour the peppermint schnapps into cup of steamin' hot cocoa and top with whipped cream.

HOT SCOTCH

2 ounces butterscotch schnapps
Hot chocolate
Whipped cream for garnish (optional)

Pour the butterscotch schnapps into an 8-ounce mug and fill it up with hot chocolate. Garnish with whipped cream if you like.

HOT TODDY

1 sugar cube or ½ tablespoon sugar
2 ounces alcohol (Bourbon or whiskey works best)
Boilin' water

Put all the ingredients in a mug and stir.

IRISH COFFEE

1½ ounces Irish whiskey
Hot coffee
Whipped cream for garnish
½ ounce Irish cream (optional)

Pour the whiskey into a mug rimmed with sugar. Fill the mug three quarters of the way with coffee, then the rest of the way with whipped cream until it is even with the rim. For added richness, add Irish cream!

OH BABY!

1 ounce butterscotch schnapps
1 ounce Irish cream
Hot chocolate
Whipped cream for garnish

Put the first two ingredients in a tall coffee mug, and fill it up with hot chocolate, stir, and top with whipped cream.

PEACH COBBLER

1½ ounces peach schnapps
6 ounces hot apple cider
Cinnamon stick for garnish

Mix the schnapps and cider in a hot drink glass. Garnish with the cinnamon stick and serve hot.

REDNECK COCOA

2 ounces Southern Comfort
1 cup hot chocolate
Whipped cream for garnish

Combine the Southern Comfort and hot chocolate in a mug and garnish with whipped cream.

FROZEN DRINKS

AMARETTO SUNRISE SLUSH

4 ounces orange juice
1 shot amaretto
½ shot grenadine
1 teaspoon lemon juice
½ cup ice cubes

Blend the orange juice, amaretto, grenadine, lemon juice, and ice cubes in blender until smooth. Pour into a tall glass.

ARKANSAS MOUTHWASH

Makes 4 drinks

5 ounces Tropical schnapps
5 ounces Mountain Dew
2 cups ice

Blend all the ingredients in a blender on high until the ice is finely crushed. It should be of a slushy consistency. Pour immediately into tall glasses and serve.

BAHAMA BREEZE

½ ounce apricot brandy
½ ounce banana liqueur
1 ounce dark rum
½ ounce coconut-flavored rum
¼ ounce grenadine
½ ounce lemon juice
1 ounce orange juice
1 ounce pineapple juice
1 teaspoon honey

Blend well with ice cubes in your blender. Pour into a tall glass.

BANANA COLADA

1 ounce dark rum
1 ounce light rum
1 banana, peeled
1 ounce coconut cream
4 ounces pineapple juice

Put all the ingredients into a blender. Blend until smooth. Serve in a tall glass.

BANANA DAIQUIRI

1½ ounces light rum
½ ounce triple saec
1½ ounces Rose's Lime Juice
1 teaspoon powdered sugar
1 medium banana, peeled
1 cup ice

Blend in your blender until smooth. Serve in a tall glass.

BANANAS FOSTER

1½ ounces spiced rum
½ ounce banana liqueur
2 scoops of vanilla ice cream
1 banana, peeled
Ground cinnamon for garnish

Blend until smooth and pour into a large brandy snifter. Sprinkle cinnamon on top.

BLENDER BOMBER

½ ounce vodka
½ ounce rum
½ ounce Jose Cuervo Gold tequila
½ ounce gin
½ ounce triple sec
1 ounce orange juice
1 ounce pineapple juice
1 ounce cranberry juice
1 ounce sour mix
¼ ounce 151-proof rum
Maraschino cherry for garnish
Orange slice for garnish

Blend all the ingredients except the rum with 1 cup crushed ice until smooth. Pour into a tall glass or mason jar and float the rum on top. Garnish with the cherry and orange slice.

BLIZZARD

1 ounce brandy
1 ounce Irish cream
1 ounce coffee liqueur

1 ounce light rum
2 scoops of vanilla ice cream
1 ounce light cream
Ground nutmeg or ground cinnamon for garnish

In a blender, blend all the ingredients until smooth. Pour into a brandy snifter and sprinkle the nutmeg or cinnamon on top.

BLUE VELVET

1 ounce Chambord black raspberry liqueur
1 ounce Midori melon liqueur
Scoop of vanilla ice cream
blue curaçao

Blend the first three ingredients until smooth. Pour into a brandy snifter and drizzle blue curaçao on top.

CHOCOLATE CAPPUCCINO SHAKE

1 ounce Irish cream
½ ounce white crème de cacao
½ ounce Kahlúa
Scoop of vanilla ice cream

Blend all the ingredients until smooth and serve in a tall glass or brandy snifter.

CHOCOLATE-COVERED STRAWBERRY

1 ounce strawberry liqueur
1 ounce Godiva chocolate liqueur
Scoop of vanilla ice cream

Blend all the ingredients until smooth and serve in a tall glass or brandy snifter.

DEATH BY CHOCOLATE

1 ounce Irish cream liqueur
½ ounce brown crème de cacao
½ ounce vodka
Scoop of chocolate ice cream
1 cup ice
Whipped cream for garnish
Chocolate kiss for garnish

Blend the first five ingredients until smooth and pour into a brandy snifter. Top with the whipped cream and chocolate kiss.

DREAM CREAMSICLE

1½ ounces vanilla liqueur
1 ounce light curaçao or orange liqueur
1½ ounces orange juice
1 ounce heavy cream

Blend the ingredients with ice until smooth and serve in a brandy snifter.

FROZEN CAPPUCCINO

½ ounce Irish cream
½ ounce coffee liqueur
½ ounce hazelnut liqueur
Scoop of vanilla ice cream
½ ounce light cream
½ cup ice
Ground cinnamon for garnish

Blend until smooth. Pour into a brandy snifter and sprinkle cinnamon on top.

FROZEN MARGARITA

1½ ounces tequila
½ ounce triple sec
1 ounce lemon juice or lime juice
1 cup ice

Blend all the ingredients until smooth. Moisten the rim of a margarita glass and dip it in salt before fillin' (page 36).

FROZEN HOP, SKIP, AND GO NAKED

Makes 4 to 6 drinks

6 ounces frozen limeade concentrate
6 ounces frozen lemonade concentrate
6 ounces peach schnapps
6 ounces Bacardi 151-proof rum

Mix all the ingredients in blender with ice to the consistency of a margarita. Serve in cocktail glasses.

IRISH CREAM MINT FREEZE

1 ounce Baileys Original Irish Cream
1 ounce peppermint schnapps
½ ounce brandy
4 ounces vanilla ice cream

Pour into a blender and mix until smooth. Pour into a tall glass or mason jar.

IRISH DREAM

½ ounce hazelnut liqueur
½ ounce Irish Cream
¾ ounce brown crème de cacao
Scoop of vanilla ice cream
1 cup ice
Whipped cream for garnish

Blend until smooth. Top with whipped cream.

ISLAND CHILLER

1½ ounces dark rum
1 ounce pineapple juice
1 ounce orange juice
1 ounce cranberry juice
1 ounce cream of coconut

Blend all the ingredients in blender with ice until smooth and serve in a tall glass.

JOCK JUICE

½ ounce peach schnapps
½ ounce apple schnapps
½ ounce strawberry liqueur
¼ ounce banana liqueur
2 ounces lemon juice
1 ounce orange juice
2 tablespoons powdered sugar
1 cup ice

Blend until smooth and serve in a tall glass.

MISSISSIPPI MUD

1½ ounces Southern Comfort
1½ ounces coffee liqueur
2 scoops of vanilla ice cream
Whipped cream for garnish

Blend until smooth. Pour into 2 brandy snifters and top with whipped cream.

OCEAN WAVE

1¼ ounces Midori melon liqueur
½ ounce coconut rum
½ ounce light rum
1 ounce pineapple juice
1 ounce orange juice
1 ½ ounces sour mix
1 cup ice

Blend until smooth and serve in a tall glass.

ORANGE FREEZE

Makes 4 large or 2 small drinks

½ cup vodka
¼ cup rum
4 scoops of orange sherbet
½ cup orange juice

Blend all the ingredients in a blender at medium speed.

PEANUT BUTTER CUP

1½ ounces Kahlúa
1 ounce chocolate liqueur
2 teaspoons smooth peanut butter
3 ounces heavy cream
Whipped cream for garnish
Maraschino cherry for garnish

Blend with ice until smooth. Pour into a tall glass and garnish with whipped cream and the cherry.

RASPBERRY CHEESECAKE FREEZE

1 ounce white crème de cacao
1 ounce Chambord black raspberry liqueur
1 tablespoon cream cheese, Softened
2 scoops of vanilla ice cream
½ cup ice

Blend until smooth and serve in a brandy snifter or tall glass.

RASPBERRY COLADA

2 ounces Chambord raspberry liqueur
2 ounces light rum
1 ounce dark rum
3 ounces pineapple juice
2 ounces cream of coconut

Blend all the ingredients with ice until smooth. Serve in a cocktail glass or tall glass.

RUM RUNNER

1½ ounces rum
1 ounce blackberry brandy
1 ounce banana liqueur
1½ ounces fresh lime juice
½ ounce grenadine

Mix in a blender with ice until the consistency is slushy. Serve in a chilled cocktail or martini glass.

SCREAMIN' MONKEY

1 banana, peeled and cut in half
1 ounce vodka
½ ounce crème de banane
½ ounce brown crème de cacao
2 scoops of vanilla ice cream
1 ounce light cream
Whipped cream for garnish

Blend 1 banana half and the other ingredients until smooth. Pour into a large brandy snifter and top with whipped cream and the remainin' banana half as a garnish.

SLIPPERY MONKEY

¾ ounce vodka
¾ ounce coffee liqueur
1 ounce crème de banane
¾ ounce Malibu coconut rum
Scoop of vanilla ice cream

Blend until smooth and serve in a tall glass or brandy snifter.

SLOE GIN FIZZ

2 to 3 ounces sloe gin
½ ounce Homemade Sweet 'n' Sour Mix (page 147)
1 teaspoon Simple Syrup (page 148)
Club soda
Lemon slice for garnish

Mix the sloe gin, sweet 'n' sour mix, lemon juice, and syrup in a shaker, then pour into a collins glass filled with ice. Fill the glass with cold club soda and garnish with the lemon slice. Stir gently.

Chapter 9

The only thing our DJ, Mildred Brickey, likes more than mixin' songs on her dual eight-track cassette-tape sound system is settin' back and havin' a vodka stinger, a bag of Funions, and a smoke.

Mixed Drinks

I have so many personal memories of mixed drinks and multi-liquor drinks I couldn't choose a favorite to include in this chapter—in fact, most of the time I can't remember how they ended. I decided since there are thousands of mixed drinks out there to choose from, it might be better to just give you a lot more choices than to spend time with me rattlin' on. This chapter is important to me because I dearly love to concoct new inventions and love sharin' 'em with friends. Some of your favorites will be here, but a lot of these recipes are ones I have heard of and sampled in my travels on the stripper circuit, from bars and bartenders all over the country, as well as from the customers that come into the Blue Whale. Now, everybody knows there are thousands of combinations and too many to mention in just one book. If you've traveled as much as I have, or even drunk as much, or just been bar hoppin' in your own town, then you should know that it's rare that two bartenders make a drink exactly alike. You can go wild with these recipes and adjust them to suit your personal taste, or you can make 'em the way they're written here, it don't really matter to me. For example, my sister, Ruby Ann, who rarely touches a drink in public, just loves Cosmopolitans. I have included the recipe in this chapter, but since Ruby Ann doesn't like cranberry juice, I substituted grenadine for it and named the version the Rubypolitan. So whether you change 'em or not, I just hope you get as much enjoyment out of these drinks as I have, or a least think I have as best as I can remember.

Since I can't remember a real good personal story to share with you, I thought I'd give you somethin' even better. Since most of y'all are probably tired of buyin' those expensive mixes at the store, I've included a few recipes for makin' your own mixes and thrown in some of the girls at the

Blue Whale's favorite tips. I also included a drink that is a tribute to Arkansas's favorite native son and NASCAR driver called the Viagra Please! And Lord knows I have heard those words called out a lot by some of the men I have had over to my trailer.

TIPS FROM THE GIRLS

Flora LaDoushe: "Learn some fun bar tricks that you can do in between drinks to entertain the bartender. If you distract him long enough, he won't remember if you paid for that drink or not. Just make sure you put a little change on the bar next to your drink so it looks like he gave that to you.

"Avoid servin' a guest or a customer who is intoxicated . . . save it for yourself."

Edna Rotoweeder: "Avoid usin' wooden toothpicks cause they splinter, leaving wooden floaters in your drinks which will poke you in the gums.

"Do not drink on the job . . . HA!

"After you have had your way with a one-night stand, if he requests another beverage, just put a little liquor on the top of the drink and don't stir it. When he tastes the first drink he'll think it's real strong. Save the booze, folks."

Little Linda: "When you're on the fly and you're short on money for mixers, just pour your liquor in a big plastic cup and head on down to the Gas and Smokes. If you hand over your Gas and Smoke's 128-ounce Guzzler Cup for your 29¢ refill, you'll get a gallon of guzzlin' refreshment, and you can simply make your drink right there on the spot. If you need lemon, just splash in a little Mountain Dew; if you need a cherry, a little cherry cola works just fine. Besides, you can get free ice and a cocktail straw! If you pretend to slip and almost fall on your way out the door, they may even throw in a 69¢ bag of peanuts, or a day old Ding Dong. I went all the way down one time and got a $2 eight-inch pickle. I have heard this motto before when drinkin' and have made it my golden rule. Beer Before Whiskey Is Mighty Risky. Whiskey Before Beer, Never Fear.

Melba Toast: "When makin' drinks for friends at a party, make sure you pour the liquor first and then add the ice. Of course, if the party is at your trailer, fill the glass to the top with ice first, then add what little liquor you can get into the glass.

"Never shake cocktails containin' carbonated mixers or beverages. Think about it. In the bar business this is what's known as a time bomb."

Ila "Flossy" LaFleur: "Forget the bottled premixed drinks like Tom Collins or margaritas, because they have an artificial aftertaste that will put a bad taste in your date's mouth, and that's *your* job.

"Always order your liquor with juice, that way you'll also be gettin' your daily vitamins."

Ms Amy: "If your guests or customers can see you while you're mixin' their cocktails it is very important that the area you're workin' in is clean, or if it ain't, make sure that they're very very drunk.

"Only when I've got a designated driver will I drink in the car. I learned a long time ago not to have empty liquor bottles in the backseat. So instead I pour my liquor into rinsed-out shampoo bottles. The police won't say nothin' about piled up shampoo bottles in your car."

BAR TRICKS

Flora's Old Cherry Trick

Pick up a cherry and put it in the ashtray. You will need a cherry without the stem, and a brandy snifter and an ashtray. The object of this trick is that you gotta get the cherry in the ashtray without touchin' it or usin' your hands or any other part of your body to pick it up. Now, you can't just scoop up the cherry with the brandy snifter or roll it off the bar and catch it in the brandy snifter either, and you can't use a straw or spoon.

Now, this will take some practice before you try it. Place the brandy snifter open side down over the cherry. Start to rotate the snifter slowly around the cherry until you get it rolling too. When you get it goin' fast enough the centrifical force will get the cherry rollin' around up in the middle of the snifter around the walls. Then you gotta quickly flip the snifter upright and place it on the bar.

There's a Hair in My Cube

You will need two ice cubes, some salt, and two strands of human hair about six or eight inches long. Now, you tell somebody they can't pick up an ice cube with one strand of human hair. A typical person will try to tie or twist the hair around the ice cube to pick it up. But they won't be able to do it. Some might even try to get it under the ice cube and lift it. But they'll never be able to pick it up. All you've gotta do is pour a little salt on the ice cube and lay that hair over it. The ice will melt and refreeze around the hair and in a few seconds you'll be able to lift it right up.

The Old Glass Eye Trick

Ask the bartender if he's ever seen a glass eye up close and personal. If he says no or even yes, then say, "Well, let me show you mine." At that time put your hand up to your eye as if you are waitin' to snatch it from above. Now you will need to have one of those small individual milk creamers hidden in the palm of that hand. Next grab a knife or even a good strong bar straw and lift that up to you eye as well. Pretend that you're pryin' your supposed glass eye out and then say, "There we go, I almost got it." At that point in time you'll puncture the creamer with the knife or straw, lettin' that milk run all out onto the bar. Then, with that eye still closed, bring your hands down and say, "Doggone it, I hate when that happens." Give it a second or two and then open your eye and smile. Trust me, he won't remember if you paid for that last drink or not. By the way, the powdered creamer don't get 'em as good.

Well, Blow That One Out of Your Trunk

This one is easy and almost always works. Tell your bartender that you've got a few nonpersonal questions that you'd like to ask him. When he says

OK, start your questionin'. Just make sure you give him plenty of time to think about each question.

1. Think of a number between 1 and 10.
2. When you have it, multiply it by 9.
3. If the result is a two-digit number, add both the digits together to make a new number.
4. Subtract 5 from the new number.
5. Assign the correct letter from the alphabet to that number, like A if the number is 1 or B if the number is 2.
6. Think of a country that starts with the letter that you've assigned.
7. Spell out the country's name in your head and think of an animal that starts with the second letter in the country's name.
8. Think of the animal's color.

When the bartender says he has the color in his mind, say, "Wait a minute, sweetie, there ain't no gray elephants in Denmark."

Beer Money

Pull out a $5 bill and tell the bartender that this is his tip, but he'll have to really work for it. Ask him for an empty long-neck beer bottle. Place the $5 bill flat out on the counter and put the bottle upside down on top the bill. Now tell him if he can get the bill out from under the bottle without tippin' it over, the tip is his. And let him know he can't touch the bottle or have anyone else touch the bottle for him. Since the first thing he's gonna try is yankin' the bill out real quick, you'll want to make sure the bar is wet where you put the bill. If it ain't, sometimes it'll come right out, leavin' your bottle standin'. Now the solution to getting' that dang bill out is real easy. Simply carefully roll the bill up until it gently pushes the bottle off of it.

HOMEMADE MIXES

The following four mixes are some basics to have in your bar and under your belt.

BLOODY MARY MIX

Makes 1 gallon

2 (46-ounce) cans tomato juice
1 (10-ounce) can beef bouillon
1 teaspoon coarsely ground fresh black pepper
1 teaspoon celery salt
1 teaspoon Accent seasonin'
4 ounces lemon juice
1 (5-ounce) bottle Worcestershire sauce
Tabasco sauce to taste (for heat)

Mix all ingredients thoroughly. Refrigerate.

HOMEMADE SWEET 'N' SOUR MIX

Makes 7 cups

3 cups water
3 cups granulated sugar
2 cups fresh lemon juice
2 cups fresh lime juice

Combine the water and sugar in a large saucepan. Stir over medium heat until the sugar dissolves. Bring to a boil. Cool the syrup. Mix the syrup, lemon juice, and lime juice in a pitcher. Chill until cold. (This can be made 1 week ahead. Cover and keep chilled.)

PIÑA COLADA MIX

Makes about 8 frozen drinks or 10 drinks on the rocks

½ cup sweetened cream of coconut
½ cup half-and-half
1 cup pineapple juice

Mix all the ingredients in a blender and store in an airtight container in the refrigerator for up to 3 days.

SIMPLE SYRUP (SUGAR WATER)

1 part sugar
1 part boilin' water

Stir thoroughly until the sugar has dissolved, let cool, and pour into a clean liquor bottle. This will keep in the refrigerator for several days. (I use it to sweeten drinks without usin' granular sugar.)

ARKANSAS RAZORBACK

½ ounce rum
½ ounce vodka
½ ounce amaretto
½ ounce Kahlúa

Add all the ingredients together in a cocktail shaker with ice, shake to a froth, and strain into a cocktail glass.

ATTITUDE ADJUSTMENT

¼ ounce vodka
¼ ounce gin
¼ ounce triple sec
¼ ounce amaretto
¼ ounce peach schnapps
¼ ounce sour mix
Splash of cranberry juice

Pour all the ingredients into a shaker with ice, mix, and strain into a glass.

BACKSEAT BOOGIE

1 ounce Absolut Vodka
1 ounce gin
1 part ginger ale
1 part Ocean Spray cranberry juice
Fruit for garnish

Pour the vodka and gin into a 14-ounce glass over ice and fill it up with ginger ale and cranberry juice. Garnish with fruit and serve.

BASEBOARD STRIPPER

1 ounce gin
1 ounce rum
1 ounce vodka
1 ounce Midori melon liqueur
2 ounces pineapple juice
2 ounces sour mix
1 ounce tequila (optional)

Mix in a shaker and pour over ice into a mason jar. (This is sure to knock you to your knees.)

BIONIC BEAVER (BEN BEAVER'S FAVORITE)

12 ounces Busch beer
2 ounces Absolut vodka
2 ounces Southern Comfort
2 ounces sloe gin
2 ounces gin
2 ounces grenadine
Orange juice
7UP

Put a little crushed ice in the bottom of a pitcher, then the beer, and then the alcohol. Top off the pitcher with equal amounts of orange juice and 7UP. Stir.

BILLY MERLE'S HEART BREAKER

1 ounce strawberry liqueur
1 ounce triple sec
1 ounce dark crème de cacao
1 ounce light cream
1 ounce strawberry syrup

Pour all the ingredients into a shaker with ice, shake, then strain into a chilled martini glass.

BLUE LIGHT SPECIAL

¾ ounce apple schnapps
¼ ounce vodka
¼ ounce blue curaçao
Pineapple juice

In a shaker, mix together the schnapps, vodka, and blue curaçao. Pour into a tall glass over ice, then top it off with pineapple juice.

THE BLUE WHALE (SPECIALTY OF THE HOUSE)

1 part vodka
1 part blue curaçao
1 part orange juice
1 part pineapple juice
1 part sour mix

Pour the ingredients into a shaker over ice and mix. Pour into a tall glass or mason jar.

BLUE WHALE MARGARITA

Lime juice
Coarse salt
1½ ounces tequila
1 ounce blue curaçao
2 ounces Homemade Sweet 'n' Sour Mix (page 147)

Rim a margarita glass with the lime juice and coarse salt (page 36). Shake the tequila, blue curaçao, and sweet 'n' sour mix with ice, strain into the glass, and serve.

BUMP AND GRIND

½ ounce vodka
½ ounce gin
½ ounce rum
½ ounce triple sec
½ ounce Midori melon liqueur
2 ounces sour mix
Orange juice

Mix the first six ingredients in a shaker, pour into a glass over ice, then top it off with orange juice.

CHEF BERNIE D. TOAST'S BOURBON COBBLER

1½ teaspoons superfine sugar
3 ounces club soda
2½ ounces blended bourbon
Maraschino cherry for garnish
Orange slice for garnish
Lemon slice for garnish

In a rocks glass, dissolve the sugar in the club soda. Add crushed ice until the glass is almost full. Add the bourbon and stir well. Garnish with the cherry and orange and lemon slices.

CHOCOLATE BANANA MARTINI

2 ounces vodka
1 ounce white crème de cacao
1 ounce banana liqueur
Hershey's kiss or a Godiva chocolate for garnish

Fill a mixin' glass with the ingredients, stir, and pour into a chilled martini glass. Add a kiss or Godiva chocolate for garnish.

CHOCOLATE-COVERED MARTINI

1½ ounces vodka
½ ounce Godiva chocolate liqueur
½ ounce vanilla schnapps
Maraschino cherry for garnish

Chill a cocktail glass. Place the cherry with its stem in the chilled cocktail glass. Mix the vodka, Godiva chocolate liqueur, and vanilla schnapps. Stir, do not shake. Strain over the cherry into the glass.

CHOCOLATE MARTINI

2 ounces vodka
½ ounce crème de cacao

Pour the ingredients into a shaker filled with ice, then strain into a martini glass.

DREAMSICLE

½ ounce vodka
¼ ounce triple sec
¾ ounce DeKuyper Lemon Tattoo schnapps
½ ounce orange juice
¾ ounce half-and-half
Grenadine

In a cocktail shaker filled with ice, combine all the ingredients. Shake or stir, strain into a rocks glass, and add grenadine until it is the color of orange sherbert.

FINGER LICKIN' GOOD

1 ounce Crown Royal bourbon
1 ounce Irish cream
1 ounce butterscotch schnapps

Chill the ingredients, mix over ice, and strain into a rocks glass.

FLAMIN' BLUE BUTT KICKER

½ ounce peppermint schnapps
½ ounce Southern Comfort
½ ounce tequila
1 ounce Bacardi 151-proof rum

Layer the ingredients in a rocks glass with the rum on top. Light on fire, burn for 5 seconds, blow it out, spit on your finger, and rub around the edge of the glass to cool before drinkin'.

FLAMINGO FAN DANCER

1¼ ounces Bacardi rum
½ ounce Meyer's rum
¼ ounce Bacardi 151-proof rum
1½ ounces pineapple juice
1½ ounces orange juice
1 ounce Homemade Sweet 'n' Sour Mix (page 147)
Orange slice for garnish
Round lemon slice for garnish

Layer the ingredients in an ice-filled tall glass. Garnish with the orange and lemon slices.

FUNKY MONKEY

1 ounce rum
1 ounce crème de banane
⅝ ounce dark crème de cacao
3 ounces coconut milk
1 banana, peeled
Coconut flakes for garnish

Blend with ice until smooth. Pour into a hurricane glass and garnish with coconut flakes.

GLAUCOMA (STOP OR YOU'LL GO BLIND)

1 ounce vodka
1 ounce rum
1ounce gin
1 ounce Kahlúa
4 ounces lemon juice or Homemade Sweet 'n' Sour Mix (page 147)
1 teaspoon sugar

Pour all the ingredients into a shaker over ice. Shake well. Strain into a tall glass.

GO-GO GIRL

1 ounce Chambord
1 ounce vodka
½ cup club soda
2 ounces sour mix

Put in a shaker and show 'em what you've got! Pour into a rocks glass over ice—what else?

HAIR RAISER

3 ounces tequila
3 ounces 151-proof rum
3 ounces vodka

3 ounces gin
2 ounces amaretto

Mix all the ingredients in a hurricane glass filled with ice.

HAWAIIAN LUAU

1 ounce Midori melon liqueur
1 ounce Bacardi rum
3 ounces pineapple juice
2 ounces Sprite

Pour the melon liqueur, rum, and pineapple juice into shaker with ice and mix. Strain into a tall glass over ice, pour in the Sprite, and stir lightly.

THE HEADLINER

1 ounce Bacardi rum
1 ounce peach schnapps
½ ounce Grand Marnier
1 ounce pineapple juice
1 ounce orange juice
Maraschino cherry for garnish

Shake and strain into a collins glass filled with ice. Garnish with the cherry.

HOME WRECKER

2 ounces Midori melon liqueur
2 ounces tequila

2 ounces cranberry juice

1 ounce Jägermeister

Shake all the ingredients together and pour into a highball glass over ice. (The mornin' after this drink you'll wake up with someone who is not your wife, hence the name.)

HOT PANTS

1½ ounces tequila

½ ounce peppermint schnapps

1 tablespoon grapefruit juice

1 teaspoon powdered sugar

Shake with ice cubes and pour into an old-fashioned glass rimmed with salt (page 36).

HURRICANE

1 ounce white rum

1 ounce Jamaican rum

1 ounce Bacardi 151-proof rum

3 ounces orange juice with pulp

3 ounces unsweetened pineapple juice

½ ounce grenadine

Fruit wedge for garnish (optional)

Combine all the ingredients and mix well (shake or stir). Pour over crushed ice into a hurricane glass. Garnish with a fruit wedge if desired. (Best enjoyed through a small straw.)

ILA LAFLEUR'S COOKIE TOSSER

1 ounce vodka
2 ounces Homemade Sweet 'n' Sour Mix (page 147)
1 ounce bourbon
Drop of Kahlúa

Mix in a cocktail shaker and pour over ice into a rocks glass.

JAMAICAN SUNSET

1 ¼ ounces Captain Morgan rum
1 ½ ounces orange juice
1 ½ ounces pineapple juice
1 ounce Homemade Sweet 'n' Sour Mix (page 147)
½ ounce Meyer's rum

Shake and strain the first four ingredients into an ice-filled hurricane glass. Float the Meyer's rum on top.

LIL' LINDA'S INSTANT BREAKFAST

2 ounces Kahlúa
2 ounces vodka
6 ounces chocolate milk (Yoo-Hoo or Chocolate Soldier works best)

In a 12-ounce collins glass, put ice, mix, and enjoy!

LONG KISS GOOD NIGHT MARTINI

½ ounce Stoli Vanil
1 ounce Stolichnaya vodka
½ ounce white crème de cacao
Shaved white chocolate for garnish

Freeze a martini glass. In a shaker, put ice, the Stoli Vanil, vodka, and crème de cacao. Shake lightly and pour into the martini glass. Garnish with the white chocolate.

LUCIFER'S LAP DANCE

1½ ounces Absolut vodka
¾ ounce DeKuyper wilderberry schnapps
1 can Dr Pepper

Mix the vodka and schnapps in the bottom of a tall glass. Add ice and Dr Pepper.

MIDORI COLADA

½ ounce rum
⅓ ounce piña colada mix
⅓ ounce Midori melon liqueur
3 ounces pineapple juice
1 cup crushed ice

Just pour it all into a blender and mix until your desired consistency is achieved. Serve in a cocktail glass.

MOMMA BALLZAK'S SUMMER REFRESHER

2 ounces rum
½ cup Fresca
Ice cubes

In a glass, put the rum, Fresca, and 1 or 2 ice cubes.

MOUNTAIN SUNSET

4 ounces DeKuyper wilderberry schnapps
2 ounces vodka
12 ounces Mountain Dew
¼ ounce grenadine

Pour the schnapps and vodka into a shaker glass, add the Mountain Dew, then lace grenadine on top. Shake and pour into two tall glasses filled with ice.

OKLAHOMA TORNADO

1 ounce vodka
1 ounce Jack Daniel's
1 ounce gin
1 ounce tequila
2 ounces 7UP
1 ounce Homemade Sweet 'n' Sour Mix (page 147)

Pour all the ingredients into a mason jar and stir. Then either drink it straight from the jar or pour it into a glass and drink up.

PA-PA'S BREAKFAST BLAST-OFF

1½ ounces vodka
1 ounce triple sec
Tang to taste

First mix the vodka and triple sec in a highball glass. Add the Tang (and water if it's powdered Tang).

PEARL DIVER

½ ounce Bacardi rum
½ ounce triple sec
½ oz Midori melon liqueur
2 ounces sour mix

Pour all ingredients into a shaker and strain over ice into a rocks glass.

THE POLE DANCER

½ ounce tequila
½ ounce Midori melon liqueur
½ ounce Chambord raspberry liqueur
2 ounces pineapple juice
2 ounces orange juice
Dash of grenadine
Bacardi 151-proof rum

Combine all the ingredients except the rum, shake well with ice, pour into a highball glass, and top off with the rum.

RADIOACTIVE LONG ISLAND ICED TEA

1 ounce rum
1 ounce vodka
1 ounce tequila
1 ounce gin
1 ounce triple sec
1 ounce Chambord raspberry liqueur
1 ounce Midori melon liqueur
1 ounce Malibu rum

Pour all the ingredients over ice into a very tall glass. Sip cautiously.

RUBYPOLITAN

1 ounce vodka
½ ounce triple sec
½ ounce Homemade Sweet 'n' Sour Mix (page 147)
½ ounce grenadine
Lime wedge

Shake the liquid ingredients like hell in a shaker with ice. Place the lime wedge on the rim of a chilled martini or champagne glass. Pour the mix into the glass and enjoy!

SOMEBODY SLAPPED ME!

2 ounces Rumplemintz
2 ounces Sambuca
½ ounce Bacardi rum
2 ounces cranberry juice
3 ounces orange juice

Mix all the ingredients in a tall glass with a lot of ice, shake well, and serve. (Look out or somebody *will* slap you!)

STARDUST

½ ounce Absolut Citron
½ ounce peach schnapps
½ ounce blue curaçao
1 ounce Homemade Sweet 'n' Sour Mix (page 147)
1 ounce pineapple juice
Splash of grenadine

Fill a shaker cup with ice. Pour in all the ingredients. Shake and strain into your rocks glass.

SWEET HOME LEMONADE

1 ounce Smirnoff vodka
1 ounce gin
1 ounce Everclear or additional vodka
1 ounce light rum
Lemonade
Splash of 7Up

Mix the first four ingredients together in a tall glass with ice. Fill it up with lemonade, add the 7UP, and drink up.

WINDEX

1½ ounces tequila
1½ ounces rum
1½ ounces vodka
1½ ounces gin
1½ ounces blue curaçao
Sour mix
Splash of 7UP
Lemon wedge

Pour liquor over ice in a collins glass. Fill with sour mix and add a splash of 7UP. Squeeze a wedge of lemon in and stir.

YOU'RE IN THE DOGHOUSE, DEW

4½ ounces vodka
Mountain Dew
Lemon juice

Pour the vodka into any large cup or glass. Fill the glass with Mountain

Dew and add a few splashes of lemon juice. Add a few ice cubes, and stir. *(This one is Ruby's husband Dew's favorite drink.)*

ZOMBIE 1

1½ ounces gold rum
3 teaspoons Rose's Lime Juice
½ ounce jamaican rum
½ ounce white rum
½ ounce pineapple juice
1 ounce papaya juice
1½ teaspoons Simple Syrup (page 148)
Maraschino cherry for garnish
½ ounce 151-proof rum

Shake all ingredients except the 151-proof rum and pour over ice into a hurricane glass. Garnish with the cherry. Float the 151-proof rum at the top and light it before servin'. (Make sure your guests blow it out before tryin' to drink it or they'll *look* like zombies when they leave!)

Chapter 10

My niece Lulu Bell tries on prom dresses at Fat Fannie's Gown Emporium.
Thank the Lord, she chose to go with the taffeta caftan with matchin' flip-flops
and hair bow, instead of the little number she's modelin' in this photo.

Punches and Party Potions

If anybody knows how to have a party, it's me, and if you doubt what I'm sayin', just ask my niece Lulu Bell's graduation class. Every year the local high school, just like schools across this great land of ours, holds its traditional senior prom, where kids who've spent the past twelve to fifteen years bein' educated in math, science, English, history, and PE try to get a little lovin' or at least felt up. In order to make sure that these children don't get any further than maybe a kiss, they ask for parental volunteers to spend their evenin' in the school gymnasium keepin' a watchful eye on these semi-adults. It's their job to make sure that the kids don't get somethin' that the parents haven't gotten for a real long time themselves, if you know what I mean. Anyhow, since my brother is dead and Lulu Bell's momma is off travelin' the world with some nasty pickle salesman, my sister, Ruby Ann, told Lulu Bell that she'd be happy to be one of the chaperons for the event. Well, as y'all know, my sister keeps a pretty busy schedule and unfortunately as luck would have it, she got called away that day to Chattanooga on business. Well, Momma and Daddy had already paid the bus fare to attend an overnight church singin' over in Fort Smith, so they couldn't fill in, and Me-Ma had just gotten her annual foot scrapin' and bikini wax that mornin' so her helpin' with this function was out of the question. This meant that the only person left was me, so I got on the horn and let Melba know what was goin' on. She happily gave me the night off, so I dug under the bed and pulled out a lovely green dress, which I hand-washed in the bathtub when I bathed and hung out to dry. Since it was a real special night, I called the Gas and Smokes Convenience Store and asked Kitty Chitwood of Lot #11 if she'd drop me off a new pair of knee-highs when she got off work between 5:30 and 6:00 P.M. She said sure, so all that was left was findin' a date.

I must have spent two hours on the phone callin' numbers out of my little black notebook, only to be faced with the now obvious realization that I needed to do a little updatin' and editin' to that thing. Most of the numbers were either disconnected, no longer in service, recordin's of time and temperature from across the country, or different variations for the main AA hot line. The ones that did ring through only left me just as frustrated. You'd think that when a person dies, they'd make sure that someone called their ex-girlfriend to let her know, but as I was findin' out, that was not the case. Well, I'd spent more time on that phone than Ms. Cleo, and had had about as much luck as her as well. It looked like I'd be goin' to this prom alone. Ain't that somethin'? All these many years later after attendin' my own senior prom alone, I was about to relive history. Not a lot of people knew that I didn't have a date to take me to my prom even though I left with the entire football team when it was all over. But in all honesty, even if I'd be walkin' into that door without a man on my arm, I'd still have Mr. Glenlivet, Mr. Chivas Regal, and Mr. Smirnoff in my purse with good old reliable Mr. Everclear waitin' for me in the trunk of my car just in case I need him.

When I arrived at the over-the-toply decorated gym, I knew I was lookin' good. I'd even given myself a good burst of aerosol rose-scented air freshener, which I'd located under my bathroom sink in order to assure that I was at my peak. The lightin' in the gym was nice and low, which meant I wouldn't have to go too far under the bleachers to take an undetected snort when the time came, and trust me, it came often. By 7:30 I was feelin' no pain. But this night was not about me, but rather Lulu Bell, who looked beautiful in her taffeta caftan with matchin' flip flops and hair bow. And her date was lookin' pretty good himself. It's amazin' how nice Old Man Keaton could look once you got him out of that custodian uniform and into a suit.

Even though the music was rockin' with Polka Patty and Her Funky Accordion, it still felt like someone needed to get this party started right, and that someone was me. Pretendin' that I had a run in my knee high, I excused myself out to my car. Without a missin' a beat I'd gotten into the trunk, accidentally got locked in, got out through my backseat, opened the trunk back up, hid the bottle of Everclear under my dress, and gone back inside. I made my way over to the large bowl of fruit punch, and as I pretended to fix the streamer that was taped to the table, I poured the whole bottle in, stirred, and casually stumbled over to the nearby trash can. Smoothly I raised my leg up as if I was checkin' for hair on my feet, and let that bottle slip down my dress and into the trash can below. I felt like Honey West on that old 1960's spy TV show.

Long story short, come eight P.M. that joint was hoppin' like the Blue Whale on a Saturday night. Everybody from the student body to the faculty all the way up to the chaperones were gettin' on the dance floor. It was a cross between *Dirty Dancin'*, *Saturday Night Fever*, and *Hulabaloo*. As you can guess, it was a night to remember all around. And guess who went home with the football coach?

Sixteen years later Lulu Bell is thirty-four, Old Man Keaton has passed, and that can of rose air freshener is almost gone. But ask anyone who was there that night and they'll tell you; no one knows how to throw a party like me. Now on to the punches! The first thing you're gonna need to know is how to make an ice ring that's real pretty for your punch bowls. Just 'cause we might be cheap don't mean we ain't got no kinda class. To do this, simply fill a bundt pan or Jell-O mold about three-fourths full with water and freeze it. You can easily get it out by runnin' warm water over it for a few seconds. If you want to be fancy about it you can even put fruit or flowers in it. Make sure the doggone flowers are edible so nobody gets poisoned. I've even frozen the club soda or ginger ale that the recipe calls for, so it don't water my punch down. However, it does lose its fizz. I know you're thinkin' about it, and, yes, I tried freezin' liquor, but hard liquor don't freeze, at least not easy, and as y'all know I'm an easy kind of gal. If you mix the liquor with some of your juice it will freeze and as it melts that punch just keeps gettin' better and better!

Now if you're usin' fruit, it might sink to the bottom of your pan, so you might want to freeze half your liquid first, then add your fruit or flowers, then add the rest of your liquid and freeze again. You can also do this with ice cubes if you ain't got a Jell-O mold or Bundt pan. Come Halloween and April Fools' I like to put raisins in them cubes on account of how people mistake 'em at first for flies or critter waste. Of course at the Blue Whale the girls drink their beverages anyway on account of how we're used to findin' all kinds of foreign objects floatin' in our drinks. That's why God gave us straws.

You could freeze lemon or lime slices, strawberries, raspberries, pineapple chunks, grapes, maraschino cherries, mandarin oranges, orange slices, banana chunks, prunes, even small gifts or toys in your rings. Warnin': As we so painfully learned with Me-Ma, this may be a chokin' hazard for the feeble-minded and drunks, so please don't let 'em self-serve at the punch bowl.

Now, I highly recommend soakin' the fruit overnight in liquor and then freezin' it into your ice cubes or ring. Of course for some of y'all that are like me, you might have a problem soakin' your fruit overnight. Regardless of how tired or worn out I might be, if I've got open liquor in the fridge, I tend to find myself gettin' up in the middle of the night and suckin that container dry, even in my sleep. Yes, dear readers, I'm a sleep drinker—or somebody else has a key to my trailer home.

ARKANSAS TEA PARTY

Makes about 40 ½-cup servin's

1 liter bourbon
1 liter dry red wine
1 pint dark rum
1 pint gin
1 pint brandy
1 liter black tea
1 pint fresh orange juice
1 cup fresh lemon juice

5 ounces Simple Syrup (page 148)
Lemon peels for garnish

Mix all the chilled ingredients in a large bowl, then add a block of ice. Garnish with lemon peels.

BILLY MERLE'S SOUTHERN GIRL

Makes about 25 1-cup servin's

1 (750-ml) bottle light rum
1 (750-ml) bottle gin
1 (750-ml) bottle vodka
1 (750-ml) bottle Yukon Jack
1 (750-ml) bottle triple sec
3 cups grenadine
3 large cans frozen lemonade
2 liters 7UP

Mix the first seven ingredients in a large bowl. Add the 7UP and ice and serve in big plastic cups.

BLUE HAWAIIAN PUNCH

Makes about 20 1-cup servin's

1 (1.75-liter) bottle Malibu coconut rum
1 (1-liter) bottle blue curaçao
2 quarts pineapple juice
Homemade Sweet 'n' Sour Mix (page 147) to taste
Pineapple rings for garnish

Mix all the ingredients in a large punch bowl. Add the sweet 'n' sour mix to taste. Serve well-chilled and garnish with the pineapple rings.

BRAIN BENDER PUNCH

Makes about 25 1-cup servin's

1 fifth Everclear or vodka
1 fifth Smirnoff vodka
2 liters Mountain Dew
2 liters Surge soda
1 small bottle lemon juice
1 pint rum

Mix all the ingredients together in a punch bowl. It's best if ice is added to the punch bowl and the sodas are very cold.

CHOCOLATE MONKEY

Makes about 26 ½-cup servin's

4 cups vodka
3 cups amaretto
2 cups banana liqueur
2 cups chocolate syrup
3 cups Homemade Sweet 'n' Sour Mix (page 147)

Mix all the ingredients by shakin' well in a milk jug. Chill for at least 2 hours. Serve over ice.

COLD DUCK PUNCH

Makes 15 to 20 1-cup servin's

1 (750-ml) bottle Cold Duck champagne
1 large can frozen lemonade concentrate

2 liters ginger ale

½ gallon rainbow sherbet

Mix all the liquids in a large punch bowl. Float the sherbet on top. (Momma used to make this every New Year's Eve when Cold Duck was only 99¢ a bottle.)

DOWN-HOME PUNCH

22 to 24 1-cup servin's

1 (750-ml) bottle Jack Daniel's

1 (750-ml) bottle peach schnapps

1 quart sour mix

2 quarts orange juice

1 quart 7UP

Splash of grenadine

Mix in a punch bowl and add an ice ring to keep it cold.

EGGNOG

Makes 16 to 18 ½-cup servin's

12 eggs, separated

1 cup sugar

1 cup bourbon

1 cup cognac

3 pints heavy cream

Grated nutmeg for garnish

Usin' an electric mixer, beat the egg yolks and sugar until light in color. Refrigerate the whites for now. Slowly add the bourbon and cognac while beatin' at slow speed. Chill 3 hours. Beat the egg whites until they form soft peaks. Beat the cream until stiff. Fold the cream into the yolk mixture, then fold in the beaten egg whites. Chill 1 hour. Serve with nutmeg sprinkled on top. (If you want it a little thinner, you can add a little bit of milk or bourbon!)

FEEL LIKE A CELEBRITY PUNCH

Serves 20 if they're light drinkers and 10 if they're like me

1 (750-ml) bottle gold rum
1 (750-ml) bottle gin
1 quart grape juice
1 pint orange juice
2 quarts ginger ale
Jar of maraschino cherries
Orange slices for garnish
Lemon slices for garnish

Mix the first four ingredients in a punch bowl; add a block of ice. Add the ginger ale and cherries and their juice before servin'. Garnish with orange and lemon slices.

HAWIIAN HOOCHIE MOMMA

Makes 14 to 16 1-cup servin's

12 ounces blue curaçao
12 ounces melon liqueur
6 ounces 151-proof rum
12 ounces Absolut Citron
1 Gallon pineapple juice

Pour into a punch bowl, mix, and add a block of ice.

LOVE ME TENDER PUNCH

Makes about 25 1-cup servin's

1 (750-ml) bottle Midori melon liqueur
1 (750-ml) bottle strawberry liqueur
1 (750-ml) bottle mango liqueur

2 cups passion fruit syrup
2 large cans frozen lemonade
1 cup grenadine
2 liters 7UP or Sprite

Mix the first six ingredients in a large punch bowl, then add the 7UP. Serve over ice.

LOVE POTION #9

Makes 16 to 18 1-cup servin's

1 pint rum
1 (750-ml) bottle strawberry liqueur
1 cup passion fruit syrup
1 cup lemon juice
1 quart orange juice
1 quart lemonade

Mix all the ingredients together in a large punch bowl. Chill for 3 hours and serve over ice.

LUNCH PUNCH

Makes 16 to 20 1-cup servin's

1 (750-ml) bottle cheap champagne
4 cups light rum
2 cups triple sec
2 cups vodka
1 gallon cherry Kool-Aid
1 pint rainbow sherbet
Orange slices for garnish
Maraschino cherries for garnish

Combine all the ingredients except the sherbert in a large punch bowl. Stir, then float the sherbet on top. Garnish with the orange slices and cherries.

MOMMA'S CHAMPAGNE PUNCH

Makes 24 to 26 servin's

1 pint rum
1 fifth champagne
6 ounces frozen orange juice concentrate
6 ounces frozen pink lemonade concentrate
28 ounces pineapple juice
2 liters ginger ale
1 quart rainbow sherbert
Fruit pieces for garnish (optional)

Mix everythin' together in a large punch bowl and garnish with fruit if desired. Use an ice ring to keep it cold.

MORNIN' DEW

Makes 14 to 16 servin's

1 fifth gin
2 liters Mountain Dew
1 quart orange juice
½ cup lemon juice

Mix all the ingredients together in a gallon pitcher and refrigerate. Serve chilled.

PARTY SLUSH PUNCH

Makes about 30 servin's

1 liter light rum
10 ounces strawberries, blended
12 ounces frozen orange juice concentrate
12 ounces frozen lemonade concentrate

2 quarts brewed tea
7 cups water
1½ cups sugar
1 liter ginger ale

Put all the ingredients except the ginger ale into a container in the freezer. Stir occasionally while freezin'. Freeze to a slushy consistency and serve in glasses with a splash of ginger ale.

PIÑA COLADA PUNCH

Makes about 10 servin's

2 quarts chilled pineapple juice, divided
16 ounces chilled cream of coconut
3 cups chilled rum

Fill a Bundt pan with some of the pineapple juice and freeze it a day before makin' the punch. Pour the rest of the ingredients into a punch bowl, mix well, add the pineapple juice ring, and serve cold. The pineapple juice ring will keep the punch cold without dilutin' the flavor. You can adjust the pineapple juice/coconut cream mixture to suit your taste.

SATIN SHEETS TO CRY ON

Makes 15 12-ounce servin's

1 (750-ml) bottle Crown Royal bourbon
1 (750-ml) bottle vodka
1 pint gin
1 liter Gatorade
1 cup lemon juice
6 cans beer

Chill all the ingredients overnight. Put everything in a large container and stir. Serve in beer mugs.

SEX ON THE BEACH PUNCH

Makes 32 ½-cup servin's

1 cup peach schnapps
1 cup Midori melon liqueur
1 cup rum
1 cup Chambord raspberry liqueur
1½ quarts pineapple juice
1½ quarts cranberry juice

Mix everythin' in a punch bowl and add a block of ice.

SOUTHERN PUNCH

Makes 24 4-ounce servin's

16 ounces Southern Comfort
64 ounces Coca-Cola
12 ounces soda water
5 oranges, sliced
3 lemons, sliced
2 limes, sliced
1 jar maraschino cherries, with juice

Mix in a punch bowl, stir, and add a block of ice or an ice ring.

TRAILER PARK BRUNCH PUNCH

Makes 32 ½-cup servin's

3 bottles vodka
1 bottle peach schnapps
4 cans beer
1 quart water
1 package Tang

Put all the ingredients into a huge bowl. Stir until mixed and serve over ice.

TRAILER PARK WEDDIN' PUNCH

Makes 10 12-ounce servin's

1 large can lemonade concentrate
3 cups Absolut vodka
8 cans beer

Follow the instructions on the can of the lemonade concentrate but substitute the vodka for water. Mix well and add the beer.

TROPICAL TRASH CAN PUNCH

Makes 50 1-cup servin's

1 fifth vodka
1 fifth rum
1 fifth fruit brandy
1 fifth fruit schnapps
1 fifth Everclear or vodka
8 liters lemon-lime soda
24 ounces tropical punch Kool-Aid
Lots of assorted fruit, sliced

Start with a *clean* trash can (preferably new). Pour in and mix up all the ingredients. The fruit can be any kind—strawberries, watermelon, oranges, lemons, and limes. Have all your friends bring bottles of white liquors and different flavors of schnapps to keep it goin' all night. Keep some extra Kool-Aid and soda pop to add as your friends add their liquors.

Chapter 11

Dishwasher and food prep Dang Van Bang and assistant chef Lucille Dennis will tell you that the kitchen goes through three bottles of rum every day durin' the week, and almost twice that much on Saturday. Of course, none of the food they make has rum in it.

Rum

Our liquor salesperson, Percy Wyatt, and me have become pretty good friends over the years. We even ended up datin' for a short period of time, and, trust me, when it came to the bedroom activities, old Percy was more of a man than that hateful name his momma and daddy attached to him like a bad fish on an August day, if you know what I mean. So when I ask him questions from time to time about liquor, he's always willin' to give me some knowledgeable information as well as an occasional hickey. Now, he told me that rum is made from syrup that you get from sugarcane, or from molasses. Who knew I could've been makin' rum instead of cookies all these years?

One thing Percy didn't have to tell me is that there are three different types of rums—white, gold, and dark—'cause the good Lord and most of Arkansas knows I've seen the bottom of many of them rum bottles in my life. But what I didn't know was that they take this molasses stuff, add yeast, let it ferment for a few days, and filter it through charcoal. Then to get the dark rum, they add caramel and slap that stuff in a wooden barrel and set it aside to age. Percy went on with more unneeded information about the history of rum, which despite his nice bottom in a pair of tight-fittin' jeans reminded me why we stop datin'. Anyhow, by that time my mind was already off plannin' my own batch of elixir.

Come Sunday afternoon I was ready to make my own rum. I'd have done it on Tuesday, but after talkin' to Percy on Monday afternoon, I got too plowed and forgot about it until eleven in the evenin' on Tuesday night durin' my third set on stage, but I took a man home, and after spendin' most of Wednesday with Sheriff Gentry lookin' for my car and my good bowlin' ball, which was in the trunk, it completely slipped my mind until Thursday afternoon, but then that chicken pot pie caught on fire in the microwave, and the whole thing was nothin' but a blur till Sunday.

So I got out four quarts of molasses and boiled it. I then added four cakes of yeast—one per quart sounded about right—covered it, and let it double in size. I poured it over a dish rag I had settin' on top of the partially used charcoal remnants in my BBQ grill, allowin' it to run off into the grease trap hole down into the barrel of my ice cream maker. I divided it into two equal parts, puttin' the second portion in my hope chest, which I'd lost faith in long ago. I added caramel candies to one batch to get a good dark rum, and half a cup of suntan oil to the other to create a nice smooth coconut blend. I put both of 'em under my trailer to ferment for a week.

Unfortunately, I never got to taste any of it thanks to them dang squirrels and raccoons who somehow managed to get under my trailer and helped themselves to my private stock. They must have been under there for a long time, 'cause accordin' to animal control, they'd lost all use of their legs and most of their nervous system until just recently when they recovered in the shelter. Thanks to a recent flash flood the smell has gone away, and since the critters did up and survive, I just might be tempted to whip up another batch. Of course I got a feelin' them raccoons, which have been released back into nature, have learned their lesson and won't be comin' back, and regardless of how temptin' the aroma might be, them just-freed squirrels will probably be content to simply set up in their trees and play with their nuts.

Just in case y'all didn't catch it, I hit both my personal story and the history of rum all in one section, so don't be sendin' me no hateful e-mails or letters sayin' how I cheated you out of a section in the rum chapter. Oh, and by the way for all you animal lovers, the squirrels and raccoons are still doin' just fine, thank you, unless of course there is a full moon outside, and in that case we've learned to keep our windows and doors locked.

A DAY AT THE BEACH

1 ounce coconut rum
½ ounce amaretto
4 ounces orange juice
½ ounce grenadine

Shake the first three ingredients together and pour into a highball glass over ice. Top with the grenadine.

BAHAMA MAMA

½ ounce dark rum
½ ounce coconut liqueur
¼ ounce Bacardi 151 proof rum
¼ ounce coffee liqueur
Juice of ½ lemon
4 ounces pineapple juice

Combine all the ingredients and pour into a highball glass over ice.

BANANA COW

1 ounce light rum
1 ounce crème de banane
1½ ounces light cream
Dash of grenadine
Grated nutmeg for garnish

Shake the ingredients with ice and strain into a cocktail glass. Sprinkle nutmeg on top.

BEACHCOMBER

1½ ounces light rum
½ ounce triple sec
½ ounce grenadine
1 ounce sour mix

Shake with ice and strain into a cocktail glass with a sugared rim (page 36).

BERMUDA TRIANGLE

½ ounce spiced rum
1 ounce peach schnapps
3 ounces orange juice

Pour the ingredients into an ice-filled old-fashioned glass.

BLUE HAWAIIAN

1 ounce light rum
1 ounce blue curaçao
2 ounces pineapple juice
1 ounce cream of coconut
1 cup crushed ice
Maraschino cherry for garnish

Combine all the ingredients in a blender at high speed. Pour into a glass and top with the cherry.

CARIBBEAN LOVER

1½ ounces light rum
1 ounce amaretto
2 ounces pineapple juice

2 ounces orange juice
Splash of grenadine
Orange slice for garnish
Pineapple slice for garnish

Shake the first four ingredients together with ice and pour into a hurricane glass. Float the grenadine on top. Add the slices of orange and pineapple on top.

CHOCOLATE MINT

1 ounce light rum
½ ounce brown crème de cacao
½ ounce white crème de menthe
1 tablespoon light cream
1 teaspoon Bacardi 151-proof rum

Shake with ice and strain into an old-fashioned glass over ice cubes.

GORILLA MILK

1 ounce light rum
½ ounce coffee liqueur
½ ounce irish cream
½ ounce crème de banane
1 ounce light cream
Banana slice for garnish

Shake with ice and pour over ice into a hurricane or parfait glass. Garnish with the banana slice.

GREEN ELEPHANT

1½ ounces light rum
½ teaspoon green crème de menthe

½ teaspoon triple sec
1 tablespoon lime juice
1 teaspoon powdered sugar
Lime wedge for garnish

Shake well with ice and strain into a cocktail glass. Top with the lime wedge.

HURRICANE DONNA

¼ ounce light rum
¼ ounce gin
¼ ounce vodka
¼ ounce tequila
¼ ounce blue curaçao
Dash of cherry brandy
3 ounces sour mix
3 ounces orange juice
Round orange slice for garnish

Pour over ice into a hurricane or tall glass and stir. Garnish with the orange slice.

ITALIAN SURFER

1 ounce Malibu rum
1 ounce amaretto
Splash of cranberry juice
Splash of pineapple juice

Shake with ice and serve in a highball glass.

JACKSONVILLE CRAWLER

1 ounce light rum
1 ounce melon liqueur

3 ounces pineapple juice
Splash of grenadine

Combine the rum, melon liqueur, and pineapple juice with ice. Stir well. Pour into a collins glass and float the grenadine on top.

LITTLE DEVIL COCKTAIL

¾ ounce light rum
¾ ounce gin
1½ teaspoons triple sec
Juice of ¼ lemon

Shake with ice and strain into a cocktail glass.

LOG CABIN

3 ounces light rum
1 ounce maple syrup
1 ounce lemon juice

Shake with ice and strain into an old-fashioned glass over ice cubes.

LOOK OUT BELOW

1½ ounces 151-proof rum
Juice of ¼ lime
1 teaspoon grenadine

Shake with ice and strain into an old-fashioned glass over ice cubes.

MAI TAI

2 ounces light rum
1 ounce triple sec

Splash of crème de noyaux
Splash of grenadine
½ teaspoon powdered sugar
Juice of ¼ lime
Dash of 151-proof rum (optional)

Shake the first six ingredients with ice and strain into a tall glass about three-quarters full of ice. For a little more kick, top with a dash of 151-proof rum.

MIDNIGHT EXPRESS

1½ ounces dark rum
½ ounce Cointreau
¾ ounce Rose's Lime Juice
Splash of sour mix

Shake with ice and pour over ice into an old-fashioned glass.

MONKEY WRENCH

1½ ounces light rum
Grapefruit juice

Pour the rum into an ice-filled collins glass. Fill with grapefruit juice and stir.

NIGHTCAP

2 ounces light rum
1 teaspoon powdered sugar
Warm milk
Grated nutmeg for garnish

Put the rum and sugar into an Irish coffee glass, fill with the warm milk, and stir. Sprinkle a little nutmeg on top.

PIÑA COLADA

3 ounces light rum
3 tablespoons coconut milk
3 tablespoons crushed pineapple

Blend with 2 cups crushed ice at high speed for a short time. Strain into a collins glass and serve with a straw.

PINEAPPLE COCKTAIL

¾ ounce pineapple juice
1½ ounces light rum
½ teaspoon lemon juice

Shake with ice and strain into a cocktail glass.

PINEAPPLE FIZZ

2 ounces light rum
1 ounce pineapple juice
½ teaspoon powdered sugar
Club soda

Shake the rum, pineapple juice, and sugar with ice and strain into a highball glass over 2 ice cubes. Fill with club soda and stir.

PINK FLAMINGO

1 ½ ounces coconut rum
1 ounce amaretto
3 ounces cranberry juice
1½ ounces pineapple juice

Combine the ingredients in a hurricane glass two-thirds full of ice.

PINK PARADISE

1½ ounces coconut rum
1 ounce amaretto
3 ounces cranberry juice
1½ ounces pineapple juice
Maraschino cherry for garnish

Combine the ingredients in a hurricane or parfait glass over ice. Garnish with the cherry.

PLANTER'S PUNCH

2 ounces light rum
1 ounce Jamaica rum
2 dashes of triple sec
Juice of 1 lime
Juice of ½ lemon
Juice of ½ orange
1 teaspoon pineapple juice
Dash of grenadine

Shake first seven ingredients and pour into a collins glass filled with ice. Top with the grenadine.

RAIN MAN

1¼ ounces 151-proof rum
¾ ounce Midori melon liqueur
4 ounces orange juice

Shake and pour into a hurricane or parfait glass filled with ice.

RUM BALL

1 oz. Bacardi rum
¾ ounce Midori melon liqueur
Splash of orange juice

Shake with ice and strain into a chilled cocktail or rocks glass.

RUM COBBLER

1 teaspoon powdered sugar
2 ounces club soda
2 ounces light rum

In a glass, dissolve the sugar in the club soda. Fill the glass with shaved ice and add the rum.

RUM COLLINS

2 ounces light rum
Juice of 1 lime
1 teaspoon powdered sugar
Club soda

Shake the first three ingredients with ice and strain into a collins glass. Add several ice cubes, fill with the club soda, and stir.

RUM COOLER

½ teaspoon powdered sugar
2 ounces club soda plus more (or ginger ale) for topping off
2 ounces light rum

In a collins glass, dissolve the sugar in the 2 ounces club soda. Stir. Fill the glass with ice and add the rum. Fill with club soda or ginger ale and stir.

RUM DIDDY

¾ ounce rum
1¼ ounces pineapple juice
Dash of lemon juice

Stir with ice and strain into a chilled cocktail glass.

RUM RELAXER

1½ ounces light rum
1 ounce pineapple juice
½ ounce grenadine
Lemon-lime soda
Orange slice for garnish
Maraschino cherry for garnish

Pour the first three ingredients over ice and shake well. Pour into a hurricane or tall glass and fill with lemon-lime soda. Garnish with the orange slice and cherry.

RUM RICKEY

1½ ounces light rum
Juice of ½ lime
Club soda
Lime wedge for garnish

Pour the rum and lime juice into a highball glass over ice cubes and fill with club soda and ice cubes. Stir. Add the lime wedge.

SEWER WATER

Splash of grenadine
1 ounce 151-proof rum

½ ounce gin
¾ ounce Midori melon liqueur
Pineapple juice
Rose's Lime Juice

In a hurricane or parfait glass, splash some grenadine. Add ice, then the rum, gin, and melon liqueur. Fill with the pineapple juice and float lime juice on top.

SIDECAR

¾ ounce light rum
¾ ounce brandy
¾ ounce triple sec
Juice of ½ lime

Shake with ice and strain into a cocktail glass.

STRAWBERRY DAIQUIRI

1 ounce light rum
½ ounce strawberry schnapps
Juice of 1 lime
1 teaspoon powdered sugar
3 ounces fresh or frozen strawberries

Blend with ice in an electric blender until smooth. Serve in a tall glass.

SWAMP WATER

Splash of grenadine
1 ounce 151-proof rum
½ ounce gin
¾ ounce Midori melon liqueur

2 ounces Rose's Lime Juice

Pineapple juice

In a hurricane or big glass, splash the grenadine. Add ice, then the rum, gin, melon liqueur, and lime juice. Fill with the pineapple juice.

WAHINE WEENIE

1 ounce light rum

1 ounce vodka

½ ounce lemon juice

1½ ounces unsweetened pineapple juice

¼ ounce Simple Syrup (page 148)

Pineapple spear for garnish

Blend in a blender with 1 scoop shaved ice. Pour into a big glass. Garnish with the pineapple spear.

ZOMBIE 2

2½ ounces light rum

1 ounce Jamaica rum

½ ounce apricot-flavored brandy

1 ounce unsweetened pineapple juice

Juice of 1 lime

Juice of 1 small orange

2 teaspoons powdered sugar

1 ounce passion fruit syrup

Crushed ice

Pineapple spear for garnish

Maraschino cherry for garnish

½ ounce 151-proof rum

Blend all the ingredients except the 151-proof rum and ½ cup crushed ice at low speed for 2 minutes. Strain into a glass. Top with the pineapple spear and cherry. Carefully float the 151-proof rum on top.

Chapter 12

I don't know what drew me to Wally—his kindness, or how sexy he looked
when he had his makeup on.

Scotch

Just the smell of cheap scotch gets me all giddy inside like a young school-girl with a prom date that she ain't related to. That aroma brings back won-derful memories of a man that I truly believed would be the love of my life. His name was Wally Olsan, and he was a strappin' blond-headed rodeo clown who fell into my life back in 1998 while I was performin' my act at the Blue Whale Strip Club. When I say he "fell into my life" I mean it lit-erally. You see, Wally was legally blind, but he refused to use one of those long white canes with the red ends on 'em durin' his everyday life. God bless him, he'd walk into walls and trip over trash cans, all on account of his vanity. Mind you, he wasn't stupid. He always used the cane to help him feel his way around the corral when he was rodeo clownin'. Needless to say he was no looker. I don't know if his appearance was 'cause he couldn't see when to run or 'cause the red tip on his cane acted like a flashin' beacon to all two thousand pounds of his pure bull rivals. Whatever his looks could be attributed to didn't matter to me. For you see, dear readers, his nightly lovemakin' made up for it all (even though I did have to shout out directions from time to time for the poor blind fool).

Each night, after several Rusty Nails, Wally would treat me to the wild-est eight minutes I've ever known in my life. Yes, it was like a dream come true holdin' that hunk of a man in my arms and havin' him whisper those special scotch-tainted words so tenderly in my ear: "Yes, I love you, now shut up, I'm tryin' to concentrate." I hoped it would never end, and it probably wouldn't have if it hadn't been for Kansas City.

After that first week of livin' together, I decided to take a leave of ab-sence from the Whale to follow my love on the rodeo circuit. First stop was Jefferson City, Missouri, and it was nothin' but a good time. Wally was only thrown over the fence twice and stuck in a barrel for about an hour till they moved on to the calf ropin' competition. Needless to say, a good time was had by all for those two wonderful days in Missouri's capital city. Our next stop was to be Kansas City, but then I got word that my good friend and coworker at the Blue Whale, Little Linda, was in trouble yet again. She needed bail money, which meant the Whale's owner, Melba Toast, would be holdin' yet another benefit strip-off. What could I do but say, "Count me in." I've always been kindhearted like that. Ask anyone in Pangburn, and they'll tell you that whenever folks have been in need, I'm always the first to take my clothes off. So after a touchin' good-bye, I left my new love and headed on home. That was the biggest mistake I've ever made in my life, not countin' the time with that family of flyin' midgets and the trapeze in Salt Lake City. . . .

Gettin' back to Kansas City, while I was at The Blue Whale Strip Club shakin' my money maker for my buddy Little Linda, Wally was takin' the wrong turn onto what would wind up to be Heartbreak Avenue. Somehow he had wandered to the wrong arena in the large Kansas town, and he unknowingly, blindly took to the stage durin' a Benny Hinn Crusade. Well, before you could say hallelujah somebody had laid hands on my honeybear and healed his dumb ass. Needless to say, with his newfound vision he skipped the rodeo and came racin' back to Pangburn to share his good news with me. I was thrilled that my baby was comin' home to Momma! But somethin' happened durin' that bus trip that, even to this day, I can't explain. When he saw me, he was like a different man. He shunned my touches and kisses like I was a leper. I'd never heard him gag durin' our ten days together, but now it seemed like it was the only noise he could make. The good Lord had given him his sight but had broken my heart. That night when I came home from the Whale, Wally, his things, and two cases of scotch (which I'd secretly stored in The High Chaparral Trailer Park storm shelter) were gone. I don't know which upset me more. I'll never get a deal like that on scotch again. But that's the way life goes when you happen to be a celebrity like myself. It's hard to hold on to the good times. And to be honest, from time to time I still resent Little Linda and her shopliftin' ways.

Lookin' for the history of how scotch is made? See the beginnin' of chapter 4.

AGGRAVATION

1½ ounces scotch
½ ounce Kahlúa
½ ounce heavy cream

Fill a rocks glass with ice, then add the scotch and Kahlúa. Top with your cream and stir.

BARBARY COAST

½ ounce scotch
½ ounce gin
½ ounce rum
½ ounce white crème de cacao
½ ounce light cream

Shake all the ingredients with ice, strain into a highball glass, and serve.

BEAGLE TAIL

1½ ounces scotch
½ ounce sweet vermouth
½ ounce dry vermouth

Stir with ice and strain into a rocks glass.

BEAVER BEND COCKTAIL

1 ounce scotch
¾ ounce Irish whiskey

Juice of ⅓ lemon
2 dashes of orange bitters

Shake with ice and strain into a rocks glass.

BIGGER'S JIGGER

2 ounces scotch
½ ounce Rose's Lime Juice
½ teaspoon superfine sugar

In a shaker half filled with ice cubes, combine all the ingredients. Shake well. Strain into a highball glass.

BLACK ROCK BLINDER

½ ounce scotch
¼ ounce Irish whiskey
¼ ounce Drambuie
1½ ounces Kahlúa

Shake with ice and strain into a rocks glass over ice.

BURNT MARTINI

1 ounce single malt scotch whisky
2 ounces dry gin

Stir with ice and strain into a chilled martini glass.

BUTTERNUT SCOTCH

1 ounce scotch
1 ounce butterscotch schnapps
1 ounce amaretto

Pour the ingredients into a rocks glass over ice and serve.

CLINTON COYOTE

1 ounce scotch
1 ounce vodka
2 tablespoons maraschino cherry juice
Splash of club soda
3 maraschino cherries for garnish

Build over ice cubes in a lowball glass. Garnish with the cherries.

DELTA DAWN

2 ounces blended scotch whiskey
½ ounce Southern Comfort
½ ounce Rose's Lime Juice
1 teaspoon superfine sugar
Orange slice for garnish
Fresh peach slice for garnish

Shake with cracked ice and pour into an old-fashioned glass. Garnish with the orange and peach slices.

DR. SCOTCH

2 ounces scotch
6 ounces Dr Pepper

Mix well in a lowball glass and add ice.

DRY ROB ROY

½ ounce scotch
1½ teaspoons dry vermouth
Lemon twist for garnish

In a mixin' glass half filled with ice cubes, combine the scotch and vermouth. Stir well. Strain into a cocktail or martini glass. Garnish with the lemon twist.

FAYETTEVILLE FLING

1½ ounces scotch
½ teaspoon Jamaican rum
Dash of orange bitters
½ teaspoon lemon juice
¼ teaspoon anisette
Maraschino cherry for garnish

Shake with ice and strain into a rocks glass. Top with the cherry.

GODFATHER

1 ½ ounces scotch
½ ounces amaretto

Pour into a glass half filled with ice, stir, and serve.

HACKETT SLING

1 teaspoon superfine sugar
2 teaspoons water
1 ounce lemon juice

2 ounces scotch
Lemon twist for garnish

In a shaker half filled with ice cubes, combine the sugar, water, lemon juice, and scotch. Shake well. Strain into a highball glass. Garnish with the lemon twist.

HARDY HOLIDAY SOUR

1½ ounces scotch
1 ounce cherry brandy
½ ounce sweet vermouth
1 ounce lemon juice
Lemon slice for garnish

Shake all the ingredients with ice and strain into an old-fashioned glass over ice cubes. Add the lemon slice and serve.

HIGHLAND COOLER

½ teaspoon powdered sugar
2 ounces club soda plus more for topping
2 ounces scotch

Put the sugar and the 2 ounces club soda into a glass. Stir and add ice cubes and scotch. Fill with club soda, stir, and serve.

HOT POKER

2 ounces single malt scotch whisky
1½ ounces Firewater
½ ounce Tabasco sauce

Mix, add ice, and serve.

JOE COLLINS

1 ounce scotch
2 ounces Homemade Sweet 'n' Sour Mix (page 147)
Coca-Cola
Maraschino cherry for garnish

Pour the scotch and sweet 'n' sour into a collins glass over ice cubes and stir well. Fill with Coca-Cola and stir lightly. Top with the cherry and serve.

KINGSTON KILT LIFTER

1½ ounces scotch
1 ounce Drambuie
2½ ounces Rose's Lime Juice

Shake gently and pour into a rocks glass over ice.

MAN OF THE MOMENT

1½ ounces scotch
1 ounce Grand Marnier
1 ounce lemon juice
1 teaspoon grenadine

Shake with ice and strain into a cocktail glass.

ME-MA'S FLU CURE

1 pint milk
1 pint scotch

Warm the milk. Drink the scotch. Throw away the milk. Go to bed. If you are not better the next day, repeat the process.

MIAMI BEACH COCKTAIL

¾ ounce scotch
¾ ounce dry vermouth
¾ ounce grapefruit juice

Stir all the ingredients with ice, strain into a highball glass, and serve.

OZARK ORANGE JUICE

1½ ounces scotch
½ ounce triple sec
1 ounce orange juice

In a shaker half filled with ice cubes, combine all the ingredients. Shake well. Strain into an old-fashioned glass almost filled with ice cubes.

PERFECT ROB ROY

2½ ounces scotch
1 teaspoon sweet vermouth
1 teaspoon dry vermouth
Maraschino cherry or lemon twist for garnish

In a mixin' glass half filled with ice cubes, combine the scotch and vermouths. Stir well. Strain into a highball glass. Garnish with the cherry or lemon twist.

ROB ROY

Dash of Angostura bitters
1½ ounces scotch
½ ounce Italian vermouth

Put bitters in a rocks glass and add ice. Add the scotch and the vermouth and stir.

RUSTY NAIL

1½ ounces scotch
1½ ounces Drambuie

Pour the ingredients into a chilled rocks glass along with several ice cubes. Stir and serve.

RUSTY SCREW

1½ ounces scotch
½ teaspoon Grand Marnier
Lemon twist

Combine the scotch and Grand Marnier in a snifter. Add the lemon twist. Sip and enjoy.

SCOTCH BOUNTY HUNTER

1 ounce scotch
1 ounce coconut rum
1 ounce white crème de cacao
½ ounce grenadine
4 ounces orange juice
Pineapple wedge for garnish
Maraschino cherry for garnish

Shake with ice and pour into a hurricane glass. Top with the pineapple wedge and cherry. Serve with a straw.

SCOTCH COOLER

2 ounces scotch
¼ ounce white crème de menthe
Club soda

Pour the scotch and crème de menthe into a glass three-fourths full of ice cubes. Fill with club soda and stir.

SCOTCH MIST

2 ounces scotch
Crushed ice
Splash of soda water

Pour the scotch over ice in a rocks glass and splash the soda water on top.

SCOTCH OLD-FASHIONED

3 dashes of bitters
1 teaspoon water
1 sugar cube
3 ounces scotch
Orange slice for garnish
Maraschino cherry for garnish

In an old-fashioned glass, muddle the bitters and water into the sugar cube, usin' the back of a teaspoon. Almost fill the glass with ice cubes and add the scotch. Garnish with the orange slice and cherry. Serve with a swizzle stick.

SCOTCH RICKEY

1½ ounces scotch
Juice of ½ lime
Carbonated water
Lime twist for garnish

Pour the scotch and lime juice into a highball glass over ice cubes. Fill with carbonated water and stir. Garnish with the lime twist and serve.

SCOTCH SQUIRT

1½ ounces blended scotch whiskey
1 tablespoon powdered sugar
1 tablespoon grenadine
Splash of Squirt

Shake the scotch, sugar, and grenadine together, then pour into a highball glass with ice. Splash on the Squirt.

SHOOTIN' THE BULL

1 ounce scotch
1 ounce dry sherry
1 teaspoon orange juice
1 teaspoon lemon juice
½ teaspoon powdered sugar

Shake with ice and strain into a rocks glass.

SILENT SERVICE

2 ounces scotch
1 ounce Cointreau
1 ounce lemon juice

Shake well with ice and strain into a rocks glass.

SMITHVILLE SURPRISE

⅓ ounce scotch
⅓ ounce Grand Marnier
⅓ ounce Peppermint Schnapps

Mix with 2 cubes of ice in a rocks glass. (Don't put in umbrellas or any of that fancy stuff.)

Chapter 13

Ms. Amy and her slug Slimy, settin' on her shoulder, are the only animal act they've ever had at The Blue Whale Strip Club, unless of course you count the time that I was performin' and a cockroach fell out of my bra.

Shooters and Shots

I'm always in the mood for a shot and even a shooter every now and then, but I got to tell y'all that when you mention those two words, I can't help but think of Ms. Amy and Slimy. That gal is about as bright as a cinder block, but she sure does try to make her numbers unique. Like the time she dressed up in a long blond wig, a beard, and a cowboy hat, and taped a feather to Slimy. She stripped to the old Sonny and Cher song "Bang Bang You Shot Me Down" in tribute to the battle of Little Big Horn. It sure was somethin' to behold.

But the time she came back from Vegas with the idea to have her pet slug Slimy jump through a hoop of fire took the cake. Now mind y'all, it wasn't a big hoop. It was just a little ol' round key chain hoop with a strip of gas-soaked cloth wrapped around it, but for this poor slug, it might as well have been the blazin' eye of a needle. We all told Ms. Amy that there was no way that slug of hers was gonna be able to jump through a hula hoop, let alone that key chain hoop. Slugs can't jump. But she had it in that little nutshell of a mind of hers that if she propelled him in the air via a little miniature teeter-totter that she'd made, he'd fly right through the flamin' hoop.

Well come show time, she proved that she was half right. Half of Slimy's little worm body made it through before comin' to rest on the burnin' ring. Luckily we had members of the volunteer fire department standin' by who, at the first sign that somethin' had gone wrong, rushed onto the stage and put out the fire. Slimy was still alive, but he was burnt. His slime-covered body had saved his life, but by the time they got to him he was all dried out. He looked like a moldy Cheeto. Quick-thinkin' Edna Rotoweeder pulled out a tube of Lanacaine, which she always keeps in her purse on ac-count of her achin' gums, and applied a light coatin' all over that poor slug's sore body. You could tell that the stuff was killin' the pain on account of the fact that his high-pitched screamin' had subsided.

Ms. Amy took her dance partner back to the dressin' room, where she gave him a good thick coatin' of Vaseline and put him in the Jell-O shot ice tray that Ila "Flossy" LaFleur keeps in the dressin' room fridge for all us gals to help ourselves to durin' those warm summer months. Flossy thought the coldness of the Jell-O would help to ease the pain that Slimy was sufferin' from, and she was probably right. Needless to say, we all was in shock. No one had thought that it would have gone that bad. We all ex-pected Slimy to go sailin' past the hoop, which was why we'd strung up a sheet to act as a safety net along the opposite side. And of course me and Flora Delight were standin' in the wings with them noodle strainers in our hands just in case he went over the bedsheet. But as I said, nobody thought he'd get burnt or hurt for that matter. That dressin' room was as quiet as morgue that night. Well, that was until Little Linda finally came into work.

She was late that night as usual, and she'd missed the drama that had unfolded before our eyes just minutes earlier. She was her old chipper self and went on and on about some man who'd taken her home the night be-fore. Of course the rest of us were in our own little world, tryin' to get those traumatic images of a slug burnin' to a crisp out of our minds. Which is why we didn't notice right away that Little Linda had opened the fridge and put a handful of Jell-O shots in her mouth. It wasn't until Ms. Amy had let out a blood-curdlin' scream that we all turned around. Ms. Amy jumped up from her chair and started poundin' on Little Linda's flabby back. I followed suit by usin' a towel as an arm extension and doin' the Heimlich on her fat behind. Before you could say "fresh and crisp" Little Linda had spit poor Slimy across the room and down Flossy's bra. He was all right, thank goodness, but in shock. After all, who wouldn't be? I can't imagine bein' burnt like a french fry, almost eaten, and then landin' in Flossy's nasty old bra. Oh, the humanity. Within a week Slimy was bet-ter and back on that stage with Ms. Amy. He sure is a trouper. All of us girls have finally gotten that nightmare out of our minds, but I know for a fact that none of us to this day will put anything in our mouths without lookin' at it first.

Back in the old western days shots were common in the saloons. Surely y'all have seen some Western movie where somebody walks into a bar and asks for a shot of liquor. Well, as the west became civilized so did the shots. By the 1900s drinkin' plain old booze became borin'; those folks wanted a real experience when it came to alcohol consumption. So they started chasin' each shot with a beer. And even though this was just the change they needed, some fool on a trolley car in St. Louis trying to impress a gal combined half a shot of gin with half a shot of milk, and to this day that shot is known around the world as the "clang, clang, clang went the trolley." Since then people have been inventin' shots and shooters that have become popular in both bars and at home.

Below y'all will find some shots and shooters that are great tastin' as well as some that are just meant to slam you to the floor like a homecomin' queen after the big game. So be careful, but enjoy!

ABSOLUTELY FRUITY

½ ounce 99 Bananas (99-proof banana liqueur)
½ ounce watermelon schnapps
½ ounce Absolut Vodka

Mix in shaker cup with ice and strain into shot glasses. Shoot, then chase with a beer.

ABSOLUTELY HOT!

Dash of hot sauce
½ ounce Absolut Pepper Vodka

Put the hot sauce in the bottom of a shot glass and add the vodka. Shoot, then chase with a beer.

AFTERBURNER

½ shot Aftershock cinnamon schnapps
½ shot Bacardi 151-proof rum

Mix in a shaker cup with ice and strain into shot glasses. Shoot, then chase with a beer.

ALABAMA SLAMMER SHOOTER

1 ounce Jack Daniel's
1 ounce crème de noyaux
1 ounce orange juice
1 ounce amaretto

Shake with ice and strain into four shot glasses. Shoot, then chase with a beer.

ANTIFREEZE

½ ounce green crème de menthe
½ ounce vodka

Shake well with ice and strain into a shot glass. Shoot, then chase with a beer.

AQUA FRESH

⅓ ounce Aftershock cinnamon schnapps
⅓ ounce Rumplemintz
⅓ ounce Avalanche peppermint schnapps

Layer by slowly pourin' each liqueur over the back of a spoon down the side of the glass one at a time—it should look like striped toothpaste. Shoot, then chase with a beer.

ARKANSAS ANTIFREEZE

⅓ ounce vodka
⅓ ounce Midori melon liqueur
⅓ ounce Homemade Sweet 'n' Sour Mix (page 147)

Shake well with ice and strain into a shot glass. Shoot, then chase with a beer.

ARKANSAS HEAD BANGER

½ ounce Jägermeister
½ ounce Goldschlager

Shake well with ice and strain into a shot glass. Shoot, then chase with a beer. (Stay away from walls.)

ARKANSAS ROADKILL

1 ounce Jose Cuervo Gold tequila
1 ounce Hot Damn schnapps
1 ounce Jack Daniel's
Coca-Cola

Pour all three ingredients into a rocks glass and serve with a Coke.

B-52 1

⅓ shot Kahlúa
⅓ shot amaretto
⅓ shot Baileys Original Irish Cream

Layer the Kahlúa, amaretto, and Irish cream in a shot glass in that order. Shoot, then chase with a beer.

B-52 2

1 ounce Grand Marnier
½ ounce Kahlúa
½ ounce Baileys Original Irish Cream

Mix the ingredients in a shaker with ice and strain into a rocks glass. Shoot, then chase with a beer.

BAILEYS CHOCOLATE-COVERED CHERRY

½ ounce Kahlúa
½ ounce grenadine
½ ounce Baileys Original Irish Cream

Layer the ingredients in order by pourin' each slowly over the back of a bar spoon into a shot glass. Shoot, then chase with a beer.

BALD KNOB BULLDOG

1 ounce rum
1 ounce Jose Cuervo Gold tequila
1 ounce Jägermeister
1 ounce Seagram's 7 Whiskey
1 ounce peppermint schnapps

Shake with ice and strain into 5 shot glasses. Shoot, then chase with a beer.

BANANA BOOMER SOONER SHOOTER

1 ounce rum
1 ounce banana liqueur
1 ounce lemon juice
1 ounce orange juice
1 ounce pineapple juice

Shake with ice, strain into 5 shot glasses, shoot, then chase with a beer.

BEAMER SCREAMER

1 shot Aftershock
1 shot Jim Beam

Fill a shaker half full with ice cubes. Pour the ingredients into the shaker and shake well. Strain into 2 shot glasses. Shoot, then chase with a beer.

BLACK HOLE

½ ounce Jägermeister
½ ounce Rumplemintz

Make certain that the ingredients are as cold as possible. Pour the Jägermeister into a shot glass and top with the Rumplemintz. The Rumplemintz will sink to the bottom, givin' a black hole effect. Shoot, then chase with a beer.

BOILERMAKER

1½ ounces blended whiskey
12 ounces beer

Pour the whiskey into a shot glass and drop into a mug of beer. Some folks say to get the full effect, you got to chug it down fast!

BODY ROCKER

1 ounce Jägermeister
1 ounce Goldschlager
1 ounce Irish whiskey
1 ounce Jack Daniel's

Layer the ingredients equally into 4 individual shot glasses in order. Shoot, then chase with a beer.

BOY HOWDY!

Serves about 12

4 ounces amaretto
4 ounces Southern Comfort
2 ounces Yukon Jack
2 ounces Rose's Lime Juice

Mix all the ingredients in a shaker with ice. Shake for approximately a minute, till really cold. Pour into shot glasses. Shoot, then chase with a beer.

BRAIN FREEZE

2 ounces Jose Cuervo Gold tequila or Bacardi 151-proof rum
Small (12 ounces) cherry slush from a convenience store machine
    (Those cola slushes will work too.)

Pour in the tequila and stir with a straw. Drink it quick and you are guaranteed a brain freeze.

BRAVE BULL SHOOTER

4 dashes of Tabasco sauce
½ ounce tequila

Pour the Tabasco sauce into the bottom of a shot glass and add the tequila. Shoot, then chase with a beer!

BUBBLEGUM

1 ounce vodka
½ ounce Banana Liqueur
½ ounce peach schnapps
2 ounces orange juice

Shake with ice and strain into shot glasses. Shoot, then chase with a beer.

BUTTER CUP

½ ounce Irish Cream, cold
½ ounce butterscotch schnapps, cold

Layer in a shot glass. Shoot, then chase with a beer.

CAM SHAFT

1 ounce Irish cream
1 ounce Jägermeister
1 ounce root beer schnapps

Chill over ice, strain, and serve as a shot in a rocks glass. Shoot, then chase with a beer.

COLORADO KOOL-AID

½ shot amaretto
½ shot Southern Comfort
½ shot cranberry juice
Splash of grenadine

Shake all ingredients with ice and strain. Shoot, then chase with a beer.

CORDLESS SCREWDRIVER

½ ounce Everclear or 100-proof vodka
½ ounce orange juice

Pour into a shot glass so that the OJ rests on top. Put your hands behind your back and pick up the glass usin' only your mouth and shoot. Then chase with a beer.

DELAYED REACTION

1 ounce 151-proof rum
1 ounce Jose Cuervo Gold tequila
1 ounce Jägermeister

Pour into a shaker with ice. Shake and serve strained into shot glasses. Shoot, then chase with a beer. (Don't worry, your taste buds will grow back in a day or two. They get easier to drink after you've had a couple. Be prepared for a delayed reaction—usually 20 minutes.)

DOGGONE IT!

1 ounce Crown Royal bourbon
1 ounce beer
3 dashes of Tabasco sauce

In the order given, pour into a rocks glass. Shoot, then chase with a beer and enjoy.

EDNA ROTOWEEDER'S JELL-O SHOTS

1 (.35-ounce) box Jell-O, any flavor
1 cup boilin' water
1 cup vodka, rum, or Everclear

Dissolve the Jell-O in the boilin' water, add the alcohol, and stir. Pour into shot glasses or those 1-ounce plastic cups found at party supply stores. (We use medicine cups from the nursin' home.) Chill until firm. People can use their tongues to loosen the edges of the Jell-O and then suck 'em down. Keep 'em on ice so they'll stay cold longer. Use all kinds of flavors!

EVIL TONGUE

1 ounce Tanqueray gin
1 ounce Midori melon liqueur
Splash of sour mix
Splash of 7UP

Pour all the ingredients into a shaker over ice. Shake and strain into 2 shot glasses. Shoot, then chase with a beer.

FIREBALL

1½ ounces cinnamon schnapps, cold
Tabasco sauce

Pour the schnapps into a shooter glass and add as much Tabasco sauce as you can stand. Shoot, then chase with a beer.

FLAME OF LOVE

⅓ ounce amaretto
⅓ ounce grenadine
⅓ ounce Bacardi 151-proof rum

Pour the amaretto then the grenadine into a tall shot glass. Pour the rum slowly so that it rests on top. Light it with a match or lighter. Let it burn for 5 seconds, then blow it out. Stink in your straw and suck it down fast. Then chase with a beer

FLAMIN' ARMADILLO

½ ounce Jose Cuervo Gold tequila
½ ounce amaretto
¼ ounce 151-proof rum

Pour the tequila and amaretto into a large shot glass. Float the rum and light it with a match. Blow it out and suck it down with a straw. Then chase with a beer.

FLAMIN' DR PEPPER

10 ounces beer
1 ounce amaretto
½ ounce 151-proof rum

Pour the beer into a large beer mug (make sure there is room—it will foam up). Pour the amaretto into a shot glass and float the rum on top. Light the shot and drop it into the beer, shot glass and all. Chug the drink before it foams over. Chase with more beer.

FLAMIN' DR PEPPER 2

½ ounce amaretto
¼ ounce Kahlúa
⅛ ounce root beer schnapps
¼ ounce 151-proof rum
6 ounces beer

In a shot glass, pour the amaretto, Kahlúa, and schnapps. Float the rum on top. Fill a mug halfway with the beer. Light the shot on fire, drop it into the beer mug and slam it as fast as you can! The faster it's slammed, the more it tastes like Dr Pepper. Chase with more beer.

FLAMIN' IDIOT

½ ounce whiskey
½ ounce amaretto
Dash of Everclear or vodka
8 ounces beer

Pour the whiskey and amaretto into a shot glass. Top the shot with Everclear. Light the shot on fire and drop it into a glass of beer. Chug! But watch out!

FOURTH OF JULY SHOOTER

⅓ ounce grenadine
⅓ ounce vodka
⅓ ounce blue curaçao

Pour the ingredients carefully over back of a bar spoon into a shot glass so that each ingredient floats on the precedin' without mixin', then shoot. You'll see fireworks after a few of these, so chase with a beer.

FROG IN A BLENDER

¾ ounce Midori melon liqueur, cold
¼ ounce Irish cream, cold
4 dashes of grenadine

Pour into a shot glass and shoot, then chase with a beer.

FUNKY CHICKEN

½ ounce Jose Cuervo Gold tequila
½ ounce Wild Turkey

Mix in a shot glass. Serve and do the chicken dance. Then chase with a beer.

FUZZY NO NAVEL

1 ounce Absolut Vodka
½ ounce peach schnapps

Pour the vodka then the schnapps into a shot glass and shoot with a beer chaser. (Keep both bottles in the freezer.)

GOLD RUSSIAN

½ ounce vodka
½ ounce Galliano

Pour into a shot glass, shoot, then chase with a beer.

GORILLA

½ ounce Bacardi 151-proof rum
½ ounce Jägermeister

Pour over ice into shaker, strain into a shot glass, shoot, then chase with a beer.

GRAPE KOOL-AID

Makes 4 shots

½ ounce blue curaçao
1 ounce cranberry juice
½ ounce pineapple juice
½ ounce Southern Comfort
⅕ ounce Homemade Sweet 'n' Sour Mix (page 147)
⅕ ounce Chambord

Combine all the ingredients in a shaker with ice and strain into shot glasses.

GREAT BALLS OF FIRE

½ ounce Goldschlager
½ ounce cinnamon schnapps
½ ounce cherry brandy

Layer in a tall shot glass or rocks glass. Shoot, then chase with a beer.

HAWAIIAN PUNCH

1 ounce Southern Comfort
1 ounce sloe gin
1 ounce orange juice
1 ounce amaretto

Shake with ice, then strain into 4 shot glasses. Shoot, then chase with a beer.

HEARTBREAK HOTEL

⅓ ounce amaretto
⅓ ounce Irish cream
⅓ oz. DeKuyper Peachtree Schnapps

Layer in order to drink to your old loves. Shoot, then chase with a beer.

HOLY HAIL

1 ounce pepper vodka
5 dashes of Tabasco sauce
Splash of tomato juice

Mix all the ingredients in a shaker with ice and strain into a shot glass. Shoot, then chase with a beer.

HONEY-DEW-ME

½ ounce vodka
½ ounce Midori melon liqueur
Splash of orange juice

Mix all the ingredients in a shaker with ice and strain into a shot glass. Shoot, then chase with a beer.

HORNY BULL

½ shot Jose Cuervo Gold tequila
½ shot Southern Comfort

Pour into a shot glass, shoot, then chase with a beer.

HUNKA-HUNKA BURNIN' LUV

½ ounce vodka
½ ounce Hot Damn schnapps

Pour the chilled ingredients into a shot glass, shoot, then chase with a beer.

HURTS SO GOOD!

½ ounce Aftershock cinnamon schnapps
½ ounce Goldschlager

Mix together in rocks glass. Shoot, then chase with a beer.

IGUANA BITE

1 ounce Jose Cuervo Gold tequila
¾ ounce triple sec
½ ounce vodka
1¾ ounces orange juice
1¾ ounces sour mix
Splash of 7UP

Mix the ingredients and shake with ice. Strain and pour into 2 shot glasses.
Shoot, then chase with a beer.

JASPER GOES JAMAICAN

1¼ ounces Jamaican rum
¾ ounce crème de banane
¾ ounce pineapple juice
¼ ounce grenadine

Shake with ice and strain into a rocks glass. Shoot, then chase with a beer.

KAMIKAZE

1 ounce vodka
1 ounce triple sec
½ ounce Rose's Lime Juice

Shake with ice and then strain into rocks glasses. Shoot, then chase with a beer.

KICK ME

½ ounce Jägermeister
½ ounce Jack Daniel's
½ ounce Jose Cuervo Gold tequila
½ ounce Firewater

Shake with ice and then strain into a rocks glass. Shoot, then chase with a beer.

KLINGON CLOAKIN' DEVICE

⅓ ounce bourbon
⅓ ounce tequila
⅓ ounce cinnamon schnapps

Pour into a shot glass and shoot, then chase with a beer.

LAVA

½ ounce Firewater
½ ounce Everclear or vodka
5 drops of Tabasco sauce

Put all the ingredients into a shot glass and shoot, then chase with a beer.

LEMON DROP

1 shot vodka
Sugar
Lemon wedge

Chill the vodka over ice, then strain into a shot glass. Sprinkle sugar on the lemon wedge. Down the vodka and bite into the lemon. Then chase with a beer.

LOUNGE LIZARD

1 ounce vodka
½ ounce melon liqueur
½ ounce Cointreau
Splash of light cream

Shake with ice and strain into 2 shot glasses. Shoot, then chase with a beer.

MARMADUKE MEMORY LOSS

2 ounces rum
1 ounce Jose Cuervo Gold tequila
1 ounce amaretto

Mix all the ingredients in a shaker glass with ice. Pour into 4 shot glasses. Shoot, then chase with a beer.

ME-MA IN A WHEELCHAIR

1 ounce Grand Marnier
½ ounce tequila
½ ounce 7UP
Splash of Rose's Lime Juice

Add ice. Shake it. Strain it. Shoot it.
Pour all ingredients in a shaker with ice, strain into a rocks glass, and shoot with a beer chaser.

MIGHTY DEW

1½ ounces 151-proof rum
Splash of Mountain Dew

Shake with ice and strain into a shot glass. Shoot, then chase with a beer.

MUD SLIDE

⅓ ounce vodka
⅓ ounce Kahlúa
⅓ ounce Irish cream

Pour all the ingredients into a shot glass, shoot, then chase with a beer.

NITRO

⅓ ounce brandy
⅓ ounce Sambuca
⅓ ounce Goldschlager

Mix all the ingredients in a shot glass and shoot with a beer chaser.

ORGASM

Serves 8

2 ounces vodka
2 ounces amaretto
2 ounces Kahlúa
2 ounces light cream

Mix the ingredients with ice in a shaker and strain into 8 shot glasses. Shoot, then chase with a beer.

PANGBURN PITBULL

1 ounce Jim Beam
1 ounce amaretto
1 ounce sloe gin
1 ounce Irish cream
1 ounce lemon-lime soda

Pour all the ingredients into a shaker with ice. Strain into shot glasses, or you can shake without ice and pour over ice into a rocks glass. Makes 5 shots or one large shooter.

PARAGOULD POND SCUM

1 ounce peach schnapps
1 ounce Midori melon liqueur
1 ounce Meyer's dark rum
½ ounce milk

Pour the peach schnapps into a martini glass. Then pour the melon liqueur over the back of a bar spoon slowly so that it rests on top of the peach schnapps. Then layer the rum on top of the melon liqueur. Fill a bar stirrer or straw halfway with the milk. Add drops of it into the glass. The milk should spread out like "scum." Shoot with a straw and chase with a beer.

PASSED OUT NAKED ON THE BATHROOM FLOOR (AKA THE LITTLE LINDA)

¼ ounce Rumplemintz
¼ ounce Jägermeister
¼ ounce Jose Cuervo Gold tequila
¼ ounce Bacardi 151-proof rum

Shake with ice and strain into 2 shot glasses. Shoot, then chase with a beer.

PEACH NEHI

¾ ounce vodka
¾ ounce peach schnapps
¾ ounce DeKuyper Cheri-berri Pucker
Splash of sour mix
Splash of pineapple juice
Splash of 7UP

Shake with ice and strain into 4 shot glasses. Shoot, then chase with a beer.

PIGGOT PITBULL

1 ounce Jose Cuervo Gold tequila
1 ounce Jägermeister
1 ounce Jim Beam
1 ounce Bacardi 151-proof rum

Shake with ice and strain into 4 shot glasses. Shoot, then chase with a beer.
(Guaranteed to make you think a dog got a hold of you!)

PINEAPPLE UPSIDE-DOWN CAKE

½ ounce Irish cream
½ ounce vodka
½ ounce butterscotch schnapps
½ ounce pineapple juice

Shake with ice and strain into 2 shot glasses. Shoot, then chase with a beer.

PRESTONE

2 ounces Midori melon liqueur
2 ounces Absolut Citron
1 ounce pineapple juice
Splash of Sprite

Pour the ingredients over ice and strain into 6 shot glasses. Shoot, then chase with a beer.

PUCKER UP

Splash of 7UP
1 ounce DeKuyper Sour Apple Pucker Schnapps
1½ ounces vodka

Add all the ingredients to an ice-filled shaker. Shake and then strain into a rocks glass. Shoot, then chase with a beer.

RATTLESNAKE BITE

1 ounce tequila, chilled
1 ounce tomato juice
Dash of black pepper
Dash of Tabasco sauce

Pour the tequila and tomato juice into a rocks glass. Top with the pepper and Tabasco sauce and shoot. Chase with a beer.

SALEM'S REVENGE

⅓ shot Jose Cuervo Gold tequila
⅓ shot Jack Daniel's
⅓ shot Goldschlager
Several drops of Tabasco sauce

Combine in order in a shot glass and shoot! Then chase with a beer.

SCOOBY SNACK

¾ ounce Malibu coconut rum
¾ ounce Midori melon liqueur
1 ounce pineapple juice
½ ounce half-n-half

Shake the ingredients in a mixin' cup with ice. Strain into a rocks glass and serve. Shoot, then chase with a beer.

SHOTGUN WEDDIN'

½ ounce Jim Beam
½ ounce Jack Daniel's
½ ounce Wild Turkey

Pour the Jack Daniel's and Jim Beam into a rocks glass, then float the Wild Turkey on top. Shoot, then chase with a beer.

SILVER SPIDER

½ ounce vodka
½ ounce rum
½ ounce triple sec
½ ounce crème de cacao

Shake with ice and strain into 2 shot glasses. Shoot, then chase with a beer.

SIP AND GET FUNKY

1 ounce gin
3 ounces beer
½ ounce grenadine
½ ounce 7UP

Mix the ingredients, pour into a rocks glass, and slam it. Chase with a beer.

SKID MARK

½ ounce coffee liqueur
½ ounce Jägermeister
½ ounce Rumplemintz

Shake with ice and strain into a rocks glass. Shoot, then chase with a beer.

SLAP SHOT

¾ ounce vodka
¼ ounce banana liqueur
Splash of pineapple juice
Splash of orange juice

Shake with ice and strain into a shot glass. Shoot, then chase with a beer.

SMACK OVER SOOTHER

2 ounces amaretto
2 ounces melon liqueur
1 ounce vodka
1 ounce sour mix

Mix all the ingredients in shaker glass with ice. Strain into 6 shot glasses. Shoot, then chase with a beer.

SNAKEBITE

½ ounce Jack Daniel's
½ ounce Jose Cuervo Gold tequila
Tabasco sauce, to taste

Pour the Jack Daniel's and tequila into your shot glass. Then add a few (5 to 10) drops of Tabasco sauce and shoot with a beer chaser.

SNEAKER

½ ounce Chambord raspberry liqueur
½ ounce Malibu coconut rum
½ ounce Bacardi 151-proof rum
½ ounce Midori melon liqueur
½ ounce cranberry juice
⅕ ounce 7UP

Shake with ice and strain into a rocks glass. Shoot, then chase with a beer.

SOUTHERN PINK FLAMINGO

½ ounce Southern Comfort
½ ounce Malibu coconut rum
½ ounce pineapple juice
Splash of grenadine
Splash of lemon juice

Mix all the ingredients in a shaker glass with ice. Strain into 2 shot glasses. Shoot, then chase with a beer.

STILETTO

⅓ ounce Kahlúa
⅓ ounce peppermint schnapps
⅓ ounce Jose Cuervo Gold tequila

Layer in a shot glass and shoot. Then chase with a beer.

TEST TUBE BABY

½ ounce amaretto
½ ounce tequila
2 dashes of light cream

Pour the amaretto and tequila into a shot glass. Drop the cream into the center. Shoot, then chase with a beer.

TEXARKANA RATTLESNAKE

1 ounce Yukon Jack
½ ounce cherry brandy
1 ounce Southern Comfort
Splash of Homemade Sweet 'n' Sour Mix (page 147)
Splash of grenadine

Mix all the ingredients in a shaker glass with ice. Strain into 3 shot glasses. Shoot, then chase with a beer.

TEXAS TETANUS SHOT

1 ounce grain alcohol
Dash of grenadine
1 ounce vodka
1 ounce rum
1 ounce gin
1 ounce Jose Cuervo Gold tequila

Mix all the ingredients in a shaker glass with ice. Strain into 5 shot glasses. Shoot, then chase with a beer.

THREE-LEGGED MONKEY

1 ounce Crown Royal bourbon
1 ounce amaretto
1 ounce pineapple juice

Shake with ice and strain into a rocks glass. Shoot, then chase with a beer.

TRACTOR PULL

½ ounce Galliano
½ ounce Southern Comfort
½ ounce Jim Beam

Mix all the ingredients in a shaker glass with ice. Strain into a shot glass. Shoot, then chase with a beer.

VIAGRA PLEASE!

½ ounce Jack Daniel's Tennessee Whiskey
½ ounce tequila
5 to 10 drops Tabasco sauce

Put 1 part whiskey and 1 part tequila into a shot glass. Then add a few drops of Tabasco sauce. Shoot it, and have some beer!

WILD WILD WEST MEMPHIS

1½ ounces Jack Daniel's
1 ounce peach schnapps
2 ounces cranberry juice

Mix all the ingredients in a shaker glass with ice. Strain into a rocks glass. Shoot, then chase with a beer.

YOOHAW

1½ ounces whiskey
½ ounce Yoo-Hoo

Pour half the whiskey in a shot glass, then top with half the Yoo-Hoo. Shoot, then repeat. Then chase with a beer

ZIPPER HEAD

⅓ ounce vodka
⅓ ounce Chambord raspberry liqueur
⅓ ounce club soda

Mix and serve in a chilled shot glass. Chase with a beer.

Chapter 14

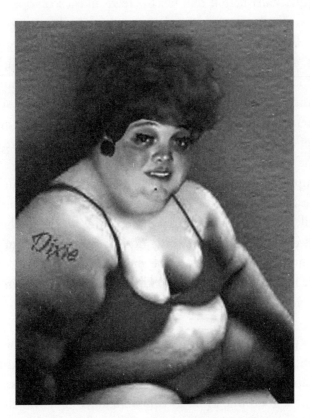

God bless her, Little Linda is the Blue Whale's very own Robert Downey, Jr. I don't mean that Robert's a 300-and-some-odd-pound woman who drinks tequila like it was Orange Crush and hides Ding Dongs and Suzy Q's in her bra, but simply that they've both had their run-ins with the law.

Tequila

Little Linda, who is a dear friend, a wonderful drinkin' buddy, and an avid lover of tequila, can't help it that her life reads like a soap opera on Valium. If her taste in food was as bad as it is in men, she'd be a size two, if you know what I mean. And the poor thing just seems to have nothin' but drama goin' on in her life. And she's a hoot to be around, but I'll tell y'all, if I didn't look so dang thin standin' next to her, I'd end our friendship right here and now. Don't get me wrong, she don't cramp my style or try to steal my men, like some gals have in the past (Faye Faye LaRue, just to name one of those old thievin' evil cows), but I just don't like all the baggage that she tends to carry with her.

For example, one evenin' about six years back at the Blue Whale, we were doin' a boomin' business at the bar, and had even been doin' exceptionally well on the Fish Basket sales, accordin' to the kitchen staff that night, so all the gentlemen were full and in great spirits. I am always glad to see 'em eat a good meal before the show. So many of 'em can't seem to handle their liquor and run to the bathroom to get sick durin' the performance. Havin' a good meal before we go on can help calm their rowdy guts.

We had a pilots' convention in town, so there were a lot of strangers in the house and obviously with all those boys flyin' out the next mornin' the booze was flowin', and they were ready to bring on the girls. We knew it was gonna be a good one as far as tips went since they was all linin' up to use the dollar changer. Plus I'd even gone out and played with several of 'em. I'd go up to 'em, wink, and as I fiddled with their hair I'd teasingly ask, "Coffee, tea, or me." You'd be surprised at how many pilots like tea.

Billy Merle had just started bartendin' behind the bar that evenin'. He liked to free-pour liquor instead of measurin' it, which was just fine by me. He said in a place like this with entertainers like us, he felt the customers should get their money's worth if not more when it comes to the booze. It was nice to know he was lookin' out for the customers like that; I thought he must have been a *manager* at his last job with the kind of good business sense that he had.

(Of course if Melba or Bernie had been there that night, they'd have told him to cut back on the amount of booze he was puttin' in those drinks, but they was away in Vegas enjoyin' a contest trip they'd won at the White County Fair. They'd had to guess how many night crawlers were in an aquarium. The contest ended on the last day of the fair, but it took them till almost Halloween to get 'em all counted 'cause they keep escapin' So, while Melba was gettin' a demonstration on a new vacuum cleaner–floor scrubber–sewin' machine–soda fountain all in one, her husband, chef Bernie, was calculatin' how to win that trip to Vegas for a three-night stay at the home of the Mega-Dog, the Westward Ho Hotel and Casino.)

Now, everyone was havin' a good time and the loose change was flowin' like water. That first set had been so good that all us gals could talk about in the dressin' room as we got rested was how the second set should be even better since they'd be even more drunk (for all you non–show people, a set is when each gal goes on for one or two numbers). As we all chatted away, Little Linda came flyin' into the dressin' room, knockin' over cocktails and dress racks as she usually does with her wide girth. But I could tell somethin' was up her craw and that she was mad. She was huffin' and blowin' like a whale on the beach by the time she reached my station. I told her to sit down and take a few deep breaths while I mixed her up a cocktail out of the personal bar I keep under my garter belt drawer. I was mortified to find all I had left was tequila. I made myself a note to stop by Beaver Liquor and Wines on my way into work the next day so I could re-stock my bar. There ain't nothin' worse then bein' out of booze and havin' to go and heist some hooch from the main bar. Anyhow, I mixed us up a couple of Memory Eliminators usin' my Big Gulp cup as a mixin' glass and a chopstick as my stirrer. I always keep a clean knee high around to strain the ice out of my drinks 'cause as far as us gals are concerned, ice takes up too much room in the glass and dilutes the booze, if you know what I mean.

Little Linda is a big gal who, when upset, tends to pace or get violent. And at her size any amount of unneeded movement can easily mean that somethin' of yours will more than likely get broken or severely damaged. So I wanted to kind of calm her down, and I made her take a few swigs of her cocktail in an attempt to settle her nerves before I asked her any kind of questions. When I finally felt the time was right, I asked her what was goin' on.

Accordin' to Little Linda, the boyfriend that she'd been seein' for the past month and a half had once again broken his promise to her. He swore that after he had enough money to buy her a ring, he'd marry her. It seemed that she was lookin' forward to bein' a June bride, but tonight, while enjoyin' a few drinks and our show, he said he didn't have the money to buy her a ring right now and the weddin' would have to wait until he got another big coast-to-coast load. Of course she noticed that he'd had the money to buy himself a brand-new gold pocket watch. And she said that after he passed out at the table and she'd gone through his wallet, she found a picture of him with some new girl. Well, we all knew he was drunk—after all, he was tippin' Flossy dollar bills for goodness sake. So Little Linda finished off her drink and as she tried to get to her feet, she said she was tired of bein' lied to by that son of a gun, and she'd fix his wagon. She marched out the back door and we didn't see her again until it was time for her number.

When closin' time came around, I helped Little Linda carry her man back to his rig. I don't know what drinks she'd been pourin' down his throat, but by the time the Blue Whale closed, I don't think he could remember his own name. Anyhow, after Little Linda assured me that she had a ride home, me and the man of my dreams for that night headed back to my trailer home in Lot #6 over at the High Chaparral Trailer Park.

The next afternoon when I woke up, you can imagine my surprise when I turned on the boob tube and heard that while Little Linda's boyfriend had been sleepin' it off in his rig, he was robbed. They got his wallet, his gold watch, and had even broke into his trailer and stolen a bunch of his load, which he was haulin' to a brand-new Holiday Inn over in Durant, Oklahoma. Well, I jumped on the horn and called Little Linda to make sure she was all right. It took several tries before she answered the phone on account of how she claimed to have been up until five in the mornin'. She must have had a hard time tryin' to fall asleep on account of those boyfriend problems. Anyhow, she said she had not seen the news yet, but that she was just fine. I told her that if she needed anything to call me or I'd just see her tonight. I kind of wished I hadn't talked so long on the phone with her on account of the fact that when I hung up I realized that my one-night stand had managed to unlock the bedroom door with one of my bobby pins, find his shoes and pants, and sneak out the bathroom window.

That night after makin' a pit stop at Beaver Liquors and Wines, I came into work and back to the dressin' room, where I dropped my two boxes of liquor off on my makeup station. I noticed right away that all the gals were grinnin' from ear to ear, but I couldn't fiqure out what was goin' on. Then it hit me. Right there next to my table was a brand new minibar. Come to find out, Little Linda, who I guess was depressed over her jackass of a boyfriend, had gone out and got all us gals minibars. Plus she had several large landscape paintin's that had bolts with 'em so you could bolt 'em to your wall. And if that wasn't enough, she also gave us a bunch of tiny bottles of shampoo, conditioner, lotion, and mouthwash, along with a few small bars of soap and some shoe shine cloths. It was like Christmas back there in that dressin' room that night. We sure was grateful, even though we couldn't quite figure out how Little Linda had managed to get all those minibars and such all the way from her place to the bar. She said that she borrowed a friend's Subaru Outback and just tied things on all over the top of the car. Boy, I'd sure would have liked to see that.

On account of the recent crime wave that was hittin' that part of town (not only had someone broken into that man's rig, but somebody stole one of my boyfriends the night before while I was dancin' up onstage), I went over to Lamb's Super Store and bought one of them tall safes so I could install it in my station and lock up my minibar when I ain't in the dressin' room. Boy, I tell y'all, I don't know how Little Linda transported those items in that Subaru, 'cause that safe alone in my trunk had my Bonneville draggin' the road.

As far as Little Linda and that trucker, well, she ended it the next day. Accordin' to her, she don't want no man who can't deliver his load as promised. And speakin' of his load, they still ain't found one item that was stolen. Accordin' to Sheriff Gentry, that stuff has probably been sold on the black market and is somewhere over in Russia by now. Thank goodness I got my safe.

We have the Spaniards—not the dogs, but the people—to thank for inventin' tequila. But before tequila was invented the Aztec people were makin' a fermented concoction from a plant called the agave. Back then it was illegal to be intoxicated, so they only let the old and sick people and nursin' mothers drink it. I bet a lot of people were sick all the time, or nursin', especially on Saturday night. This Saturday tradition continues even to this day.

Tequila was also used in religious rituals, which makes me wonder where the religious people got the idea that drinkin' was wrong. Anyhow, the Spaniards came along and decided to change the taste, so they fermented it and gave it the name *mezcal*. Still the Spaniards drank mostly water—the dogs, not the people this go 'round.

Mezcal (mescal) can be made from several different agave plants, not to be confused for a cactus, which ain't gonna give you diddly-squat. But tequila can be made only from the blue agave plant. Mr. Jose Cuervo was the first to get permission from the government to start cultivatin' and producin' tequila, but it was Cenobio Sauza who first started sendin' it to America. To this day most of the premium brands of tequila are still produced in Mexico. American-made tequila is usually mixed with cane alcohol to make it cheaper, so it ain't real 100 percent agave tequila—but try tellin' that to a worm.

Your basic types of tequila are silver, gold, and *añejo*, which is aged for at least one year but no more than five years. Tequila also don't need to age to get better, it's usually as good as it's gonna get right when it's made; however, some companies age it anyway. For me personally, I don't mind waitin', but on the other hand I've been known to suck one of those blue agave plants bone dry. One night I thought after work I thought I saw a blue agave plant in my sister's front yard. Needless to say, I picked that thing up and started suckin' like there was no tomorrow, you know, since that night I can't recall seeing another porcupine at The High Chaparral Trailer Park. Well, a girl does get thirsty! And don't worry, I didn't hurt that poor sleepin' thing, even though it did run back into the woods without a quill left on its tiny body.

ACAPULCO BREEZE

1½ ounces gold tequila
¾ ounce Cointreau
2 ounces pineapple juice
1½ ounces orange juice
¼ ounce grenadine

Shake all the ingredients with ice. Pour into a chilled, sugar-rimmed margarita glass (page 36).

ACAPULCO LOCO

1½ ounces tequila
½ ounce triple sec
½ ounce rum
Splash of sour mix

Shake all ingredients in a cocktail shaker, strain into a rocks glass, and serve.

ALAMO REFRESHER

1½ ounces tequila
1 ounce orange juice
½ ounce pineapple juice
Splash of 7UP

Pour over ice into a tall glass and stir.

BAJA BANANA BOAT

1½ ounces tequila
1 ounce banana liqueur
½ ounce Galliano
1 ounce light cream

Shake with ice and strain into a chilled martini glass.

BIG HOT HOOTER

1 ounce tequila
¾ ounce amaretto
3 ounces pineapple juice
1 ounce grenadine

Pour the tequila and amaretto into a highball glass filled with ice. Fill it with pineapple juice and top with the grenadine.

BLOODY MARIA

1½ ounces tequila
Dash of Worcestershire sauce
Dash of Tabasco sauce
Dash of salt and pepper

Dash of lime juice
Tomato juice

Pour the first five ingredients over ice into a tall glass, then fill it with tomato juice.

BLUE MARGARITA

1½ ounces tequila
¾ ounce. blue curaçao
4 ounces sour mix

Blend with ice and strain into a chilled margarita glass with a salted rim or pour over ice into a rocks glass with a salted rim (page 36).

BRAVE BULL

1¼ ounces tequila
¾ ounce Kahlúa

Build over ice in a rocks glass and stir.

BREACH OF PROMISE

½ ounce tequila
½ ounce Goldschlager
½ ounce Jack Daniel's

Pour in order into a shot glass.

BULL RIDER

1½ ounces tequila
1 ounce coffee liqueur
Lemon twist for garnish

Pour into a glass with ice and stir. Top with the lemon twist.

CACTUS JUICE

1 ounce tequila
1 ounce amaretto
2 ounces Homemade Sweet 'n' Sour Mix (page 147)

Pour into a rocks glass and stir.

CANCUN REFRESHER

1½ ounces tequila
¼ ounce triple sec
3 ounces cranberry juice
1 ounce pineapple juice
½ ounce orange juice
Lime wedge for garnish

Pour the first three ingredients into a glass of ice and stir gently. Top with the pineapple and orange juices. Add the lime wedge.

DEW RIGHT BABY

½ ounce tequila
½ ounce dark rum
½ ounce vodka
½ ounce triple sec
½ ounce melon liqueur
Mountain Dew

Put the first five ingredients into a tall glass with ice, top it off with Mountain Dew, and stir.

DOWNSHIFTIN' DEMON

2 ounces tequila
1 ounce Bacardi 151-proof rum
2 ounces fruit punch-flavored Kool Aid
1 ounce Sprite

Pour into a plastic cup over ice.

DRUNKEN MONKEY

1 ounce tequila
Splash of orange juice
Dash of lemon juice
½ banana, peeled

Blend with crushed ice; serve in a highball or decorative glass.

FREDDY FUDDPUCKER

1¼ ounces tequila
4 ounces orange juice
½ ounce Galliano

Pour the tequila and orange juice into a highball glass over ice. Float the Galliano on top.

GRAND GOLD MARGARITA

1¼ ounces Jose Cuervo Gold tequila
¾ ounce Grand Marnier
3 ounces sour mix

Shake with ice and serve on the rocks or strain into a chilled salt-rimmed margarita glass (page 36).

HORSESHOE BENDER

1 ounce tequila
1 ounce Southern Comfort
1 ounce Wild Turkey
5 ounces orange juice
½ ounce grenadine

Pour the first four ingredients into a tall glass over ice and top with grenadine.

HOT PANTS

1½ ounces tequila
1½ ounces peppermint schnapps
½ ounce Hot Damn schnapps

Shake with ice cubes and pour into a chilled martini glass.

MARGARITA

1½ ounces tequila
¾ ounce triple sec
Splash of sour mix
Squeeze of lime juice

Shake with ice and serve on the rocks or strain into a chilled salt-rimmed glass (page 36).

MARGARITA PEACHY BLUE

1½ ounces tequila
2 ounces peach schnapps
1 ounce blue curaçao
4 ounces sour mix

Shake with ice and strain into a chilled margarita glass.

MEMORY ELIMINATOR

1½ ounces tequila
1½ ounces Wild Turkey 101
6 ounces Orange Crush soda

Mix all the ingredients in a tall glass with ice.

MEXICAN MELONBALL

2 ounces tequila
2 ounces Midori melon liqueur
2 ounces sour mix
Splash of orange juice

Shake and pour into a tall glass with ice.

MIDORI MARGARITA

1 ounce tequila
½ ounce triple sec
1 ounce Midori melon liqueur
1½ ounces sour mix

Shake with ice and pour into a chilled margarita glass.

MONKEY SWEAT

1 ounce tequila
½ ounce banana liqueur
½ ounce triple sec
6 ounces pineapple juice

Shake the ingredients together and pour into a glass with crushed ice.

OCEAN WAVE

1 ounce tequila
½ ounce triple sec
½ ounce Malibu rum
⅛ ounce blue curaçao
1½ ounces Homemade Sweet 'n' Sour Mix (page 147)
Lime slice for garnish

Shake all the ingredients with ice and strain into a chilled cocktail glass. Garnish with the lime slice.

PEACH MARGARITA

1 ounce tequila
1 ounce peach schnapps
2 ounces Homemade Sweet 'n' Sour Mix (page 147)

Shake with ice and strain into a chilled margarita glass.

PERFECT MARGARITA

1½ ounces Sauza tequila
1 ounce Cointreau
Juice of ½ lime
Juice of ½ lemon

Shake with ice, strain, and serve up in a chilled, salt-rimmed margarita glass (page 36).

POINTS OF PLEASURE

1 ounce vodka
1 ounce tequila
1 ounce Yukon Jack

2 ounces cranberry juice
2 ounces orange juice
2 ounces pineapple juice

Pour in a hurricane glass with ice and stir.

PUCKER UP, RITA

¾ ounce tequila
½ ounce Dekuyper Sour Apple Pucker Schnapps
1 ounce sour mix or lime juice

Shake with ice and strain into a chilled margarita glass.

RODEO RIDER

1 ounce tequila
1 ounce Kahlúa
1 ounce whiskey
1 ounce beer
1 ounce Mountain Dew

Combine in a tall glass over ice.

SILK STOCKIN'

1½ ounces tequila
1 ounce crème de cacao
1½ ounces light cream
Dash of grenadine
Ground cinnamon for garnish

Shake all the ingredients with ice and strain into a chilled cocktail glass. Sprinkle the cinnamon on top.

SIMPLY DEWLIGHTFUL

1 ounce tequila
1 ounce vodka
1 ounce Kahlúa
4 ounces fruit punch-flavored Kool Aid
1 ounce Rose's Lime Juice
Splash of Mountain Dew

Mix the first five ingredients in a shaker and pour over ice. Top with the Mountain Dew.

STRAWBERRY MARGARITA

1 ounce tequila
½ ounce triple sec
Splash of sour mix
3 ounces frozen strawberries
Dash of grenadine

Blend with crushed ice until thick and smooth. Serve in a chilled margarita or tall glass.

STRIPPER'S ZIPPER

2 ounces tequila
1 ounce orange curaçao
1 ounce Chambord raspberry liqueur
1 ounce vanilla syrup
2 ounces coconut milk
2 ounces pineapple juice

Shake and pour into a tall glass over ice.

TEQUILA MOCKINGBIRD

1½ ounces tequila
½ ounce triple sec
2 ounces orange juice
1 ounce cranberry juice
½ ounce blue curaçao

In a highball glass filled with ice, add the tequila, triple sec, and orange and cranberry juices. Top with blue curaçao.

TEQUILA SUNRISE

1½ ounces tequila
4 ounces orange juice
½ ounce grenadine

Pour the tequila and orange juice into a highball glass over ice. Top with the grenadine.

TEQUILA SUNSET

1 ounce tequila
Orange juice
½ ounce blackberry brandy

Pour the tequila into a tall glass filled with ice. Fill with orange juice and stir well. Top with blackberry brandy and stir lightly.

TIJUANA TAXI

2 ounces Gold tequila
1 ounce blue curaçao
1 ounce tropical fruit schnapps
7UP
Orange slice for garnish
Maraschino cherry for garnish

Pour the first three ingredients into a highball glass and fill with 7UP. Garnish with the orange slice and cherry.

TIJUANA TEMPTATION

1 ounce tequila
1 ounce Absolut Vodka
1 ounce banana liqueur
1 ounce Irish cream

Mix in a shaker and pour over ice in a highball glass.

WILD THING

1½ ounces tequila
½ ounce Rose's Lime Juice
1 ounce cranberry juice
2 ounces club soda
Round lime slice for garnish

Pour into a highball glass with ice and stir. Top with the lime slice.

Chapter 15

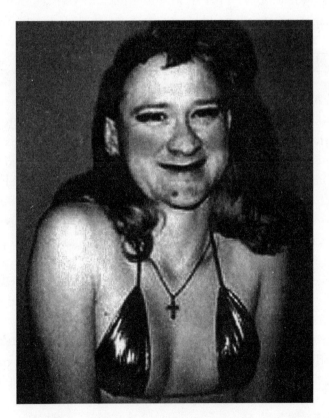

Vodka drinker and fellow dancer Edna Rotoweeder says that the folks at the insurance swear the dentures she's been waitin' a little over a year for will arrive before Christmas. Yeah, and Santa will be bringin' them himself.

Vodka

God bless her, my dear friend and fellow Blue Whale girl Edna Roto-weeder ain't got a tooth in her head, but after four vodka collinses she can eat corn right off the dang cob and even faster than most folks I know who've got a full set. And after six of these adult vodka beverages, she could take a set of lug nuts off a tire with those gums of hers. It ain't like she's talented with her mouth or nothin', like I happen to be (I can dismantle a tractor with my lips when the spirit hits me), but rather it's all on account of the vodka and what it does to her. This ain't unusual. There are many folks that feel the effects of the clear intoxicatin' juices in several different ways. Some get loud or mean, while others become great big old pussycats. Others, like Edna, get superhuman strength, but unfortunately she can't drink it all the time on account of what else it does to her. You see, even after just one simple shot of vodka poor Edna gets some of the worst flatulence that's ever filled the air. And it goes on for hours. The sad part is that she loves the stuff. And of course, Melba Toast has banned her from touchin' even as much as a drop of it until the Whale has closed, the pilot light in the gas stoves in the kitchen have been turned off, and all the patrons are cleared out of the club.

And I've told her that I won't be seen in public with her if she's been hittin' the vodka either. Especially after the last time we did that tour at that winery durin' a vacation in Northern California. She'd sneaked in a few belts from a flask of vodka she had in her purse when none of us was lookin' and within minutes, the toxic fumes were goin'. Bottles of chardonnay were flyin' off the racks left and right. I'm tellin' y'all I've never been so embarrassed in all my life. Luckily for us, the fella givin' the tour thought it was some kind of gas leak and evacuated the cellar. Needless to say, Edna and I used that chance to jump in my rented Dodge Dart and head back down the coastline to our room at the YWCA in San Francisco. Of course I made Edna ride with her bottom hangin' out of the car window for the entire two hours. In all fairness, I was nice enough to draw two eyes and a nose on her butt, makin' everyone in the passin' cars think she was just smilin' at 'em rather than moonin' 'em. In any case, I can't tell you how many folks honked and waved at us that day or, for that matter, how many birds fell from the sky. When we arrived at the YWCA there was no way I was takin' her in our room since she was still as gassy as the Goodyear Blimp on a Monday night, so I took her to walk around for an hour over to Fisherman's Wharf, where we could easily blame the odor on the seafood displays that lined the streets. Now I know that some of y'all will say that I made all this up and stretched the truth about how bad the smell was. Well, if you doubt me, just go take a look at those figures in the wax museum in that part of town. They ain't been the same since.

Percy Wyatt, our liquor salesman, came into the Blue Whale one day to eat. I sat down to keep him company while he polished off the Fish Basket and I sneaked some of his fries. Just to make conversation and to make him feel special (you have to do that with men sometimes) I asked him if he knew how vodka was made. I'd heard it was made from potatoes, so I thought if it was easy, I'd try makin' some that night or whenever I thought about it again.

He told me this big long history that I didn't half care about but I humored him 'cause he was lookin' kinda cute with that new cheap dog-hair toupee he got in Mexico. If you don't get too close, so you can't see the duct tape, he kinda looks like Mr. Burt Reynolds in that movie about the stripper. Anyhow, I did catch the part that vodka either came from Poland or Russia, I don't really remember which, but in one of them countries they drank it with meals. Percy acted like that was somethin' surprisin'. I think most people drink somethin' with their meals. I happen to like vodka, too, or rum, or scotch, or whatever might be handy in my bar at the time. They also chase it down with a soft drink or beer. He told me there is an old Russian sayin' that "vodka without beer is money thrown in the wind." Even though I didn't understand it, I couldn't agree more with our Russian comrades! By the way, someday me and the girls hope to take our show to Russia, Poland, and other Slavic countries—if they ever tear down that wall.

I remember he also said vodka was originally made for medical purposes, so I figure that it must have some kind of healin' power. After all, I never get sick on it. He also told me that in Russia it was believed to contain its own spirit, so they used it at religious events. If a person didn't drink it he was considered unholy. If that's the case, I must have a Rolls-Royce and a penthouse suite waitin' for me in heaven. However, dear sweet Edna's got a chain of hotels and a cruise ship with her name on 'em.

Well after all that, Percy never did tell me how to make vodka, so I tried to concoct it myself by runnin' some potatoes thru my Mr. Juicer, which I took as a trade-in at my store The Real Easy Pawn, to see what would happen. I tried several ways to get it to ferment, and found the closest came when I added a bottle of rubbin' alcohol (the big bottle). It even began to taste like vodka after about an hour of samplin' and three more batches from the Mr. Juicer. If I hadn't passed out, I'm sure that in time I'd have unlocked the secret to that sacred Russian recipe.

APPLE MARTINI

1 ounce vodka
2 ounces Dekuyper Sour Apple Pucker Schnapps
Dash of Homemade Sweet 'n' Sour Mix (page 147)

Shake and strain into a chilled cocktail glass.

ARKANSAS KOOL-AID

1 ounce vodka
2 ounces Southern Comfort

1 ounce peppermint schnapps

6 ounces fruit punch–flavored Kool Aid

1 ounce Rose's Lime Juice

Pour all the ingredients into a shaker glass with ice. Shake and then pour over ice into a mason jar.

BIG JOHNSON

4 ounces vodka

4 ounces Jack Daniel's

¾ can 7UP

Dash of lime juice

½ ounce grenadine

Mix the first four ingredients in a large highball glass over ice. Pour the grenadine on top and stir.

BLACK RUSSIAN

1½ ounces vodka

1 ounce coffee liqueur

Pour into a glass half filled with ice and stir well.

BLOODY BULL

1 ounce vodka

2 ounces tomato juice

2 ounces beef bouillon

Lime slice for garnish

Stir all the ingredients in a glass half filled with ice and top with the lime slice.

BLUE LAGOON

1 ounce vodka
1 ounce blue curaçao
Lemonade
Maraschino cherry for garnish

Pour the first two ingredients into a glass half filled with ice. Fill with lemonade and top with the cherry.

BLOODY MARY

1½ ounces vodka
3 ounces tomato juice
Dash of lemon juice
1 teaspoon Worcestershire sauce
2 to 3 drops Tabasco sauce
Sprinkle of salt
Dash of pepper
Celery stick

Shake with ice and strain into a glass two-thirds full of ice cubes. Add the celery stick to stir with.

CAJUN MARTINI

3 ounces vodka
Dash of dry vermouth
Large jalapeño pepper for garnish

Mix the vodka and vermouth with ice, stir briskly, and strain into a chilled cocktail glass. Garnish with the jalapeño.

CAPE COD

1½ ounces vodka
4 ounces cranberry juice
1 ounce Homemade Sweet 'n' Sour Mix (page 147)
1 teaspoon Simple Syrup (page 148)

Mix the ingredients in a shaker and strain over ice cubes into a chilled old-fashioned glass.

CARIBBEAN CRUISE

1 ounce vodka
½ ounce light rum
½ ounce coconut rum
Splash of grenadine
4 ounces pineapple juice
Pineapple wedge for garnish
Maraschino cherry for garnish

Shake all the ingredients except the pineapple juice with ice and strain into a glass two-thirds filled with ice. Fill with the pineapple juice. Top with the pineapple wedge and cherry.

COLORADO BULLDOG

1 ounce vodka
1 ounce Kahlúa
2 ounces milk
Splash of Coca-Cola

In a shaker, mix the vodka, Kahlúa, and milk. Pour into a rocks glass and add a splash of Coca-Cola.

COSMOPOLITAN MARTINI

1½ ounces vodka
1 ounce cranberry liqueur

Pour all the ingredients into a mixin' glass half filled with ice, shake well, then strain into a martini glass.

CRAWFORDSVILLE COOLER

1½ ounces citrus vodka
¾ ounce triple sec
1 ounce melon liqueur
2 ounces sour mix
Lemon-lime soda

Pour first four ingredients into a hurricane glass filled with ice cubes. Fill with soda and stir well.

DESERT SUNRISE

1¼ ounces vodka
2 ounces pineapple juice
1½ ounces orange juice
Dash of grenadine

Shake all the ingredients and pour into a glass filled with crushed ice.

DEW-DRIVER

2 ounces vodka
1 ounce orange juice
Mountain Dew

Fill a highball glass with ice, add the vodka and orange juice and fill it up with Mountain Dew.

DR PEPPER MARTINI

1 ounce vodka
1 ounce triple sec
2 ounces Dr Pepper

Stir with cracked ice. Strain into a chilled cocktail glass.

DR. SCREW

2 ounces vodka
4 ounces orange juice
Dr Pepper

Pour the vodka and orange juice into a glass half filled with ice cubes and stir well. Then top it off with the Dr Pepper.

ELECTRIC JAM

1¼ ounces vodka
½ ounce blue curaçao
2 ounces sour mix
Lemon-lime soda

Pour into a glass two-thirds full of ice and stir.

EXTRA DRY VODKA MARTINI

¼ ounce dry vermouth
2 ounces vodka

Pour the vermouth into a mixin' glass, swirl it around, and pour it out. Add ice to the mixin' glass, then the vodka. Gently stir with a plastic spoon or stick (not metal) for 1 minute. Strain into a prechilled martini glass.

FRENCH MARTINI

1½ ounces vodka
1 ounce black raspberry liqueur

Pour into a mixin' glass half filled with ice, stir, and strain into a chilled cocktail glass.

FUZZY NAVEL

1 ounce vodka
½ ounce peach schnapps
6 ounces orange juice
Orange slice for garnish

Mix the ingredients with cracked ice in a shaker and pour into a chilled collins glass. Garnish with the orange slice.

GODCHILD

1 ounce vodka
1 ounce amaretto
1 ounce heavy cream

Shake well with cracked ice and strain into a champagne glass.

HARVEY WALLBANGER

1 ounce vodka
4 ounces orange juice
½ ounce Galliano

Pour the vodka and orange juice into a glass filled with ice cubes. Stir and float the Galliano on top.

ITALIAN SCREWDRIVER

1¼ ounces citrus vodka
1½ ounces amaretto
3 ounces orange juice
Splash of ginger ale
Round lime slice for garnish
Maraschino cherry for garnish

Mix and pour into a sugar-rimmed hurricane glass full of ice (page 36). Top with the lime slice and cherry.

JUNGLE JANE

1 ounce vodka
1 ounce light rum
½ ounce banana liqueur
½ ounce triple sec
1½ ounces orange juice
1 ounce cranberry juice
2 ounces pineapple juice
Splash of sour mix
Round orange slice for garnish
Banana slice for garnish
Maraschino cherry for garnish

Shake well, then pour over ice into a mason jar or hurricane glass. Top with the orange and banana slices and cherry.

MUD SLIDE

2 ounces vodka
2 ounces Kahlúa
2 ounces Baileys Original Irish Cream

Shake, then strain into a highball glass with ice.

OKLAHOMA COOLER

1½ ounces Skyy vodka
1½ ounces melon liqueur
4 ounces cranberry juice
Splash of 7UP

Mix the spirits and cranberry juice in a tall glass with ice. Add the splash of 7UP and stir.

ORANGUTAN

1 ounce vodka
1ounce 151-proof rum
½ ounce triple sec
Splash of grenadine
6 ounces orange juice
Splash of sour mix

Lightly blend all the ingredients. Strain into a large glass half filled with ice cubes.

PEACH BLOSSOM

2 ounces vodka
½ ounce peach schnapps
7UP or ginger ale

Pour the vodka and schnapps into a collins glass over ice and fill it up with 7UP or ginger ale.

PETTIGREW PARALYZER

Coca-Cola
½ ounce vodka
½ ounce Kahlúa
Milk

Fill a highball glass three-fourths of the way with Coca-Cola, add the alcohol, and top up with milk. Stir and serve.

PINK LEMONADE

1 ounce Absolut Citron
4 ounces sour mix
2 ounces cranberry juice
Splash of 7UP
Lemon slice for garnish

Shake with ice and strain into a highball glass. Garnish with the lemon slice.

PINK PUSSYCAT

1½ ounces vodka
6 ounces pineapple juice
Splash of grenadine

Pour vodka into a highball glass with ice. Fill with the pineapple juice and grenadine. (Drink should be pink!)

PURPLE PASSION

2 ounces vodka
1 ounce Chambord raspberry liqueur

Pour the ingredients into a cocktail glass, add ice, and stir.

SALTY DOG

Lime wedge
Salt
2 ounces vodka
Grapefruit juice

Rim an old-fashioned glass with the lime wedge and salt (page 36). Fill the glass with ice, the vodka, and the grapefruit juice. Stir.

SCREWDRIVER

1½ ounces vodka
5 ounces orange juice

Pour into a glass half filled with ice cubes. Stir well.

SEA BREEZE

2 ounces vodka
3 ounces grapefruit juice
3 ounces cranberry juice

Mix all the ingredients with cracked ice in a shaker and pour into a chilled highball glass.

SEX ON THE BEACH

1 ounce vodka
1 ounce peach schnapps
3 ounces cranberry juice
3 ounces pineapple juice

Add several ice cubes to a highball glass. Pour in all the ingredients and stir.

SOFT KISS GOOD NIGHT

1 ounce vodka
1 ounce creme de banane
1 ounce peach schnapps
Dash of grenadine
Squeeze of lemon

Mix with ice in a tall glass.

STUPID CUPID

2 ounces citrus vodka
½ ounce sloe gin
Splash of sour mix
Maraschino cherry for garnish

Shake with ice and strain into a chilled cocktail glass. Garnish with the cherry.

TOOTSIE ROLL MARTINI

3 ounces Absolut Vodka
½ ounce chocolate liqueur
½ ounce Grand Marnier
Orange twist for garnish

Shake with cracked ice and strain into a chilled cocktail glass. Garnish with the orange twist.

TOP BANANA

1 ounce vodka
1 ounce creme de banane
Juice of ½ orange

Shake with ice and strain into an old-fashioned glass over ice.

TOXIC WASTE

1 ounce vodka
1 ounce blueberry schnapps
1 ounce blue curaçao
3 ounces sour mix
Splash of 7UP

Shake with ice and serve in a tall glass.

TUCKERMAN TOAD

2 ounces vodka
3 ounces green crème de menthe
6 ounces Mountain Dew

Pour over ice, stir, and serve.

VIAGRA ON THE ROCKS

2 ounces vodka
1 can Red Bull Energy Drink
Dash of blue curaçao

Mix the vodka and Red Bull in a tall glass over ice. Float the blue curaçao on top.

VODKA COLLINS

2 ounces vodka
Juice of ½ lemon
1 teaspoon powdered sugar
Club soda or 7UP

Lemon slice for garnish
Maraschino cherry for garnish

Shake the first three ingredients with ice and strain into a glass one-third full of ice cubes. Fill it up with club soda or 7UP, and stir. Top with the slice of lemon and cherry. Serve with a straw.

VODKA GIBSON

3 ounces vodka
1 teaspoon dry vermouth
3 pickled pearl onions for garnish

Mix the vodka and vermouth in a mixin' glass with plenty of ice (very rapidly to eliminate the meltin' of the ice) and strain into a chilled cocktail glass. Garnish with the pickled pearl onions.

VODKA GIMLET

1½ ounces vodka
1 ounce Rose's Lime Juice
1 teaspoon powdered sugar

Shake with ice and strain into a chilled cocktail glass. Can also be served in a rocks glass with ice.

VODKA STINGER

1 ounce vodka
1 ounce white crème de cacao

Shake with ice and strain into a cocktail glass.

WHITE CHOCOLATE STINGER

1 ounce vodka
1 ounce white crème de cacao
1 ounce white crème de menthe

Shake with ice, strain into a chilled cocktail glass, and serve. It can also be served on the rocks.

WHITE RUSSIAN

2 ounces Kahlúa
1½ ounces vodka
Milk or light cream

Pour the coffee liqueur and vodka into a highball glass half filled with ice cubes and top off with milk or cream.

WILD BREW YONDER

1 ounce vodka
½ ounce blue curaçao
1 can beer

Pour the vodka and curaçao into a beer glass and top off with beer.

Chapter 16

Melba Toast, along with her husband, Chef Bernie D. Toast, is the owner of the Blue Whale Strip Club. You ain't seen sexy until you've seen Melba do a table dance after a little wine (and some help getting her and her walker up on the table).

Wines

Personally I believe that old sayin' about how elephants have long memories is very true. My sister, Ruby Ann, remembers everythin' I've ever done and often shares that information publicly. But I bring up this thing about elephants on account of how wine reminds me of the time that I rode an elephant. It was over in India and the fellow who took care of those great large beasts told me that my ridin' skills were some of the best he'd ever seen, and that I was a natural. Of course I think all that credit has to go to the fact that I dated Vance Poole for a while. But anyways, how I got to India to ride that big old thing, the elephant, not Vance, is very interestin'.

One afternoon Melba Toast, the owner of the Blue Whale, came into the dressin' room, which is better known as the Sea Cave, to talk to us gals while we was havin' our afternoon tea (Long Island Iced Tea, that is) before gettin' ready for our show. It seemed that she'd gotten a call from this fella who'd seen our show while he was on vacation and was so impressed that he asked if we'd be interested in doin' our act for his club in Bombay. Well, of course we was just thrilled and so excited that we'd actually been requested to pack up our G-strings, boas, and tassels to perform in another nation that wasn't considered a third world country. Sure, all of us have done those poor countries, but none of us had ever stripped in a real, big-time place like India before, well, not professionally that is. Without hesitation we all enthusiastically said we'd do it. Of course once we'd signed our contractual agreements for this special trip with Melba, our enthusiasm quickly cooled, 'cause it was then that she informed us that the constitution of India has a prohibition clause in it. "What?" Flora and the rest of us shouted, but before we could try to actually rise to our feet, and start swearin', Melba jumped in with a smile and said that all this means is that

276

we can't bring more than a quart of our booze into the country with us. Well, that was a little bit better, and once she assured us in writin' that we'd actually be able to get alcohol while we was there, our spirits rose again, as did our excitement. We was goin' to India, y'all.

Unsure of what lay ahead of us, me and the rest of the gals lived up to the name of Blue Whales on our international flight, 'cause we was drinkin' like fish. Heck, they had to make unscheduled stops in Memphis, Detroit, Amsterdam, and Sri Lanka just so they could restock their bar. But I blame part of our drinkin' on pure drama. Like the drama that took place when Little Linda got stuck in the bathroom with that poor little man from Bangkok, which basically says it all. God bless him, when she asked him if he wanted to join the "mile-high club," he thought she meant that he'd sign up for somethin' that let him use a special airport lounge when he traveled. You should have seen that poor feeble man when the crew was finally able to rip Little Linda out of that bathroom. I still keep that fella in my prayers even to this day, and hope that one day he'll be able to walk without that limp and back brace.

When we finally touched down, I couldn't believe how pretty it was. It was like paradise with a lot of dirt and poverty, but it was beautiful. Unfortunately I couldn't say the same about the dump they'd put us in. It was like a Motel 6 without the 6, if you know what I mean. It was bad, but that was just fine. We was only goin' to be there for two nights, and as long as it had a bed and a toilet, I was fine. Why, I'd spent the night in a motel in Tulsa that was such a dump they didn't even have a hanger, a rack, or even a hook for me to put my clothes on. Luckily I just throw 'em on the floor anyway. And that Oklahoma room was also missin' a desk, a nightstand, and any other piece of furniture where I could set my bottle. I put it on the floor at first, but after watchin' a rat and three roaches fightin' for it, I just kept it next to me in the bed. OK, so the room in India wasn't all that bad.

As promised, Melba had found us a good supply of booze. It turned out to be apple and plum wine, which I guess is easier to find than a scotch and soda in that country. Even though I wasn't a wine connoisseur, I managed to do just fine with the stuff Melba had located. It wasn't Boone's Farm by any stretch of the imagination, but it worked. And after unpackin' our clothes and costumes, and knockin' off a couple of bottles each, we gals were well rested and lubricated enough to go see this show club that we'd be performin' at. Needless to say, we was in for a surprise.

The place where we was to do our act turned out to be nothin' more than a dark dingy little banquet room that at one time had been the motel restaurant. This room had nothin'. There was no pole, no stage, and not even a tinsel curtain on the wall. Thank goodness I'd borrowed my sister Ruby Ann's gold-sequined top or we would've had to perform our entire show without a backdrop. Come to find out, Melba had misunderstood what this fella had said when he asked her to come and do our act for his club. He didn't mean for us to perform at a club he owned, which was apparent as soon as we'd walked into that dive, but rather to entertain the club he belonged to. In any case, we was all professionals—and like all professional entertainers, we believe deep down in our hearts the show must go on, period. Besides, at that point in time we hadn't yet gotten our return flight tickets from this fella. So we just hung up my sister's top, rearranged the tables and chairs so we had room to perform, checked out the strength of the tabletops, and put away another case of wine. That night we just went right to bed on account that it'd been a long day; we was gonna get up early and see the sights before the show, and Little Linda was still tuckered out from that bathroom incident and sore in places I don't dare mention in this book. I'd told those flight attendants to grease her up first so she'd slide right out, but, oh no, they didn't listen to me. It didn't matter that I'd had to pull this trick before with her at the state fair when a Porta Potti and a clown car were involved.

After a fun-filled day of seein' monkeys runnin' around a temple, enjoyin' a couple of meals that'd later bring me to tears and curse words—some of which I ain't used in years—and that elephant ride I mentioned earlier, it was time to do a show. Little Linda and I'd both been treated real nice by everyone in the streets and even though we later found out that was on account of the fact that some folks treat cows as gods in that country, we was sure we'd be loved when we took to that makeshift showroom. We'd be loved all right, but that wasn't the half of it.

Bein' the headliner and emcee, I was the first to go on. As usual, I wasn't feelin' no pain when I walked out onstage and started my number. Of course I came out to rousin' applause, but when I took off my first piece of clothin' I was surprised to hear that the audience was hissin' at me. How dare they? I wondered if they knew who in the heck I was? But bein' the professional entertainer that I am, I just kept right on goin'—to heck with these idiots, I'm a star. Of course it wasn't until the fella runnin' the giant emergency floodlight, which we'd been forced to substitute as a spotlight, had gotten so caught up in my exotic moves that he forgot to move the light when I moved across the room, that I finally got a look at my audience who were settin' in the dark. It was about twenty turbaned men settin' there with their snakes in their hands. I couldn't believe it. These guys had actually taken their snakes out and were playin' with 'em while I was on-stage bein' sexy. We'd soon find out that the club this fella belonged to was a snake charmin' club that met once a month at this hotel. Even though I happen to be a gal from the Ozarks, I don't like snakes regardless if they're in a field, a banquet room, or a church. So you can imagine that I was off that stage and out of that room faster than you could say *run*. I was later told that the men didn't know any better and had just thought it was part of my act. To fill the void, Melba Toast had rushed onstage, but once she realized that those gold slimy things tuckin' the money into her G-string weren't hands, she joined me and the case of apple wine that I was puttin' away in the motel room as well. Ila did real good on account of the fact that she couldn't see what was goin' on; however, when she got close enough to hear the hissin' from the snakes, she, too, mistook it for the men and flipped 'em off. They hated Edna on account of the fact that when she got to the part where she talks durin' her act, they thought all the lispin' she was doin' from not havin' her new teeth yet was mockery toward the snakes. She was almost bit. But the routine they loved the best was Ms. Amy and Slimy. The fellas could relate to her act, and when she pulled out her flute and played it, accordin' to Melba's husband, Bernie D. Toast, both the men and their cobras were just swayin' back and forth to the music. When that fella who'd booked us showed up with our money and tickets, he said that we'd been the best thing they'd seen since someone had brought in the DVD version of the movie *Anaconda*. He asked us if we'd please come back next year. Bein' the polite businesswoman that she is, Melba told the fella that she'd have to check our schedule when we got back home.

All in all it was a good trip. The only gal who did get bit was Flora, and if you look real close in the right light you can still see the fang marks in her wooden leg. I took a fancy to wine, me and Little Linda had a good time with the elephant handler, and I learned that the next time I want to lose a vital organ all I got to do is eat some Indian food. But still, I really don't think I'll get a chance to ride another elephant. By the way, did I mention that Vance Poole has moved into The High Chaparral Trailer Park?

I don't claim to be an authority on wine, I only know what I like, which is Reunite. In fact I don't know anyone in the trailer park that knows much about wine with the exception of Kenny and Donny over in Lot #15, Dick Inman in Lot #14, and Ben Beaver, who owns Beaver Liquors and Wines. Why, thanks to my patronage, or so Ben says, his late wife, Dora Beaver, was able to build a new luxurious wine room onto their store. It seems that they saved every penny I spent at Beavor Liquors over the last year and a half, and that was the money they used to build the "Donna Sue Boxcar Wine Room." Now, I know that sounds like I drink a lot, but y'all gotta re-member that Kenny and Donny gave 'em a 25 percent discount on all that furniture that came from the court of King Louis and Marie Antoinette, which they used to decorate the wine room with. In my opinion there are only the followin' basic types of wine, which y'all will find in either a bottle or, as I prefer, a box: white, red, rose, blush, sweet, and the ever-popular whatever's on sale.

I will give you some basics, and y'all have to go out and try some just to find out which ones you like best. I'm sure if you talk to the owner of your local wine store he can give you some pointers as to what you might like— just tell him if you like your drink to be sweet or sour.

Wines are usually named or categorized by the grapes they are made from, but they must have at least 75 percent of that type of grape in 'em to be named after it. For example, a cabernet sauvignon is made from caber-net sauvignon grapes, Mad Dog 20/20 is made from the mad grape, and Night Train is made from the Gladys Knight grape. Don't quote me on this 'cause all this information I just gave y'all I heard through the grape-vine.

Here are some brief definitions of wine types that Ben Beaver told me to put in my book. He took the time to go around his shop in that wheelchair of his and wrote notes off the bottles. If they're not right, don't blame me, blame him. Ben ain't been right for years, but I love him like a rich uncle and I'm hopin' I'm in his will, plus since he can't stand up he has trouble readin' things that are up high. Anyhow, here we go.

- Aperitifs—usually light wines like champagne, sherry, or light white wine. These are are generally served before meals.
- Blush wines—light pink wines made from several red wine grapes. Now the reason they ain't totally red is that they only have the skins of the red grapes in with 'em for a short time, which gives 'em a pink color. Blush wines are light and usually have a little bit of sweetness.
- Cabernet sauvignon—a red wine known for its deep flavor and smell. It's what they call a full-bodied wine, intense, with cherry-currant and sometimes herb flavors. It ages real good.
- Champagne/sparklin' wines—wines made sparklin' or with bubbles from the wine-makin' process. Champagnes and sparklin' wines range in style and taste from very dry to sweet. For example . . .

Natural	Very dry
Brut	Dry
Extra dry	Slightly sweet
Demi-sec	Sweet

Then there's my favorite, Spumante, which is real sweet.
- Chardonnay—a white wine that can have a variety of different tastes dependin' on the grape and the agin' process. It's a really dry wine.
- Chenin blanc—a white wine with fresh, floral characteristics, whatever that means. It grows well in warmer weather and makes a light, dry-to-not-so-dry wine.
- Dessert wines—usually served with dessert (or just skip dessert and go straight for the wine). If you're lookin' for a good dessert wine, go for sherry or port, or you might also like some sweet German wines.
- French colombard—a white wine that is usually light and slightly sweet. It is the most widely planted varietal in California.

- Fumé blanc—a white wine best known for its herbal flavors. Also called sauvignon blanc, it is a popular choice to serve with fish and other seafood dishes.
- Gewürztraminer—a white wine rich in spicy aromas and full flavors. It can be dry or even slightly sweet and is usually good with spicy dishes like Asian food.
- Grenache—a red wine grape that produces fruity, spicy wines. It also can show a lighter side and even be a little sweeter when a blush wine is made from it.
- Merlot—a red wine with medium to full body and herb flavors. Merlot is usually softer in taste than cabernet sauvignon.
- Pinot blanc—Sometimes called poor man's chardonnay because both grapes produce similar flavors and textures. They are often clear and have an intense flavor with a hint of honey and fruit.
- Pinot noir—a red wine of light to medium body and delicate, smooth, rich complexity, not nearly as heavy as a cabernet or merlot.
- Red wines—usually dry wines. They gain their color from the skin of the grape. Their taste differs because of the difference in the grapes and how the wine is aged. Cabernet sauvignon, merlot, petite sirah, pinot noir, zinfandel, and blush wines (rosés) are red wines.
- Riesling—a white wine known for its floral smell. Dependin' on where and how it's made, it can be dry as a desert or sweet.
- Rosés—also called blush wines, light pink wines made from several red wine grapes. They get their color from havin' contact with the grape skins durin' the wine-makin' process. Rosé's are light and usually have a little sweetness.
- Sauvignon blanc—also known as fumé blanc, a popular choice to serve with fish and shellfish dishes—so go back and look at fumé blanc.
- Table wines—red, white, and blush wines, They contain from 7 to 14 percent alcohol and can be made from a single variety of grapes or a combination of grapes—however the winemaker wants to mix it.
- White wines—wines ranging in style from dry to sweet. Some are aged in oak barrels.
- Zinfandel—a red wine that can be light to full bodied and has berrylike

or spicy flavors. The zinfandel grape is also widely used in makin' the white zinfandel wines that are so popular today.

Well, I hope this gives you some great ideas for you and your friends. Remember, it took years for me to acquire all the knowledge and expertise it takes to make all these delicious drinks—so don't try to overdo it. I hope you enjoy all these recipes and feel free to adjust them and change them to suit your taste. Now, of course there are some things I left out, 'cause if I share all my drinkin' knowledge this book would be as big as my Bonneville. Which means that in the near future I'll be sharin' more cocktail recipes as well as tips on throwin' the perfect parties, advice on datin', and of course keepin' you updated on the happenin's with me and the girls at The Blue Whale Strip Club.

Please don't even think about enjoyin' all of these temptin' libations in the same night, though. I don't need anyone challengin' my record. I do hope you'll drink responsibly and remember, **don't drink and drive.**

I'd suggest you select a designated driver, but that didn't work for me and the girls at the Blue Whale, for the simple reason that a slug can't drive. So instead, I recommend takin' a cab, a bus, or anything that don't put you behind a wheel of a vehicle and others in danger. The last thing I want is to lose a fan.

If you have any questions about any of the drinks in my book, or would like to share your recipes, or if you just want to talk to a star, feel free to drop me an email at Donnasuelot6@aol.com, or send your letters to Donna Sue Boxcar, in care of my publisher. You can even visit my Web site donnasueboxcar.com. I personally read and respond to every email and letter that I receive.

Thanks for readin', have fun, and remember my motto, "May your glass always be full and your bottom up!"

Index